W9-ACI-443

JOHN DRYDEN

Literary Lives
General Editor: Richard Dutton, Senior Lecturer in English,
University of Lancaster

This series offers stimulating accounts of the literary careers of the
most widely read British and Irish authors. Volumes follow the
outline of writers' working lives, not in the spirit of traditional
biography, but aiming to trace the professional, publishing and
social contexts which shaped their writing. The role and status of
'the author' as the creator of literary texts is a vexed issue in current
critical theory, where a variety of social, linguistic and psychological approaches have challenged the old concentration on writers
as specially gifted individuals. Yet reports of 'the death of the
author' in literary studies are (as Mark Twain said of a premature
obituary) an exaggeration. This series aims to demostrate how an
understanding if writers' careers can promote, for students and
general readers alike, a more informed historical reading of their
works.

John Dryden

A Literary Life

Paul Hammond
Senior Lecturer in English
University of Leeds

St. Martin's Press   New York

First published in the United States of America in 1991

Printed in Hong Kong

ISBN 0–312–05686–9

Library of Congress Cataloging-in-Publication Data
Hammond, Paul, 1953–
John Dryden: a literary life / Paul Hammond.
    p.   cm. — (Literary lives)
Includes bibliographical references and index.
ISBN 0–312–05686–9
1. Dryden, John, 1631–1700—Biography.   2. Authors, English—Early
modern, 1500–1700—Biography.   I. Title.   II. Series: Literary
lives (New York, N.Y.)
PR3423.H36   1991
821'.4—dc20
[B]   90-25288
                                                                CIP

For Martin

Contents

Prologue

Sometimes I give my soule one visage and sometimes another . . . If I speake diversly of my selfe it is because I looke diversly upon my selfe . . . I have nothing to say entirely, simply, and with soliditie of my selfe, without confusion, disorder, blending, mingling, and in one word.

Montaigne[1]

Among the manuscripts of John Aubrey in the Bodleian Library are his lives of notable contemporaries. One page is headed 'John Dryden, Esq. Poet Laureate. He will write it for me himselfe'. The remainder of the page is blank. Whatever the circumstances which deprived us of Dryden's autobiography, the silence is altogether appropriate. Dryden was a prolific writer whose contribution to the culture of Restoration England is unrivalled, and yet that copious writing eschewed autobiographical revelation. There are many statements of his critical opinions, and some of his political and religious beliefs, but it is rare to come across any disclosure of what the twentieth century (with unacknowledged irony) likes to call 'private life'. There are few intimate letters and no diary. His mode of writing often prefers several voices instead of the single voice which might be construed as authorial: he writes plays, prologues and epilogues which are spoken by actors; critical essays and religious poems in which different voices contend for mastery; translations where the voice of the translator has an ultimately indecipherable relation to the voice of the original poet. This penchant for rhetorical play is the expression of a critical and sceptical intellect which stood resolutely by certain beliefs but was always ready to probe, test and explore alternatives; it is also the self-defensive mode of the professional writer earning his living in dangerous times.

Many commentators on Dryden, from his day to ours, have traduced him with both stubborn conservatism and mercenary opportunism. In so doing they have inadequately imagined the precariousness of public life and public speech in the late seventeenth century, and neglected to consider that in any age there is no secure and privileged position outside the structures of language where a man's private self may reside. Freedom and integrity come only through a continual wrestling with and within language. The consequence of this for anyone who would write Dryden's life is that we can have no access to a secret or even stable self; there are only texts, and the interpretations which we make of them. We may make inferences about what Dryden felt and thought, but only if we acknowledge that these are simply further rewritings of our own.

The present study of Dryden's life examines the texts which he produced, considering how they engaged with their society and what notions of text and society, writer and reader they are proposing. It therefore consists of chapters on different aspects of Dryden's work; they are arranged approximately chronologically to suggest the shape of his career and to explore his own developing sense of his role as the premier writer of Restoration England, at once dominating and detached from the world in which he moved.

1

The Apprentice
1631–59

'A warlike, various, and a tragical age is best to *write of*, but worst to *write in*.'[1] This was the observation of Abraham Cowley, Dryden's favourite childhood poet, who was reflecting in 1668 on the works which he had written and failed to write during the civil war and Interregnum. Dryden's adolescence, the time when he was learning the techniques of reading and composition, mastering the ancient languages of Greece and Rome, and encountering the contemporary languages of English politics and religion, was passed during the most traumatic period of civil strife which this country has endured in modern times. The struggle for political power, for control of church and state, was won first by Parliament with the execution of Charles I in 1649, and then by Charles II at the restoration of the monarchy in 1660, but the concomitant struggle for hermeneutic power, for control over the writing of history and over the language in which the conflict was to be interpreted, has never finished. It is not only in university departments of history that the civil war is still being fought, but wherever the language of tradition, rights, freedoms and democracy is invoked. Implicitly or explicitly, the myths of our modern democracy seek its origins, if not its legitimation, in interpretations of English history from 1642 to 1688. Such an age, such a conflict, is no doubt best for us to write of, since we can choose and limit our engagement. We should therefore be specially wary of the ready application of a modern vocabulary to this period, and the imposition of easy moral judgments upon those who lived in and wrote for such a time. To be master of oneself and of one's language in a time of civil war is no simple matter. Dryden has proved to be all too easy a victim for those who think that they know what integrity must look like, and whose suave derision costs them nothing. Both speech and silence cost Dryden dear.

Peace and normality were not restored to England with the restoration of the monarchy in 1660. The delight expressed by the

1

men and women who greeted Charles II was genuine enough, as
we can see from Pepys' diary, but as we turn the pages of that
diary, and read further on into the 1660s, we soon find that Pepys
becomes dismayed at the way in which the country is being
governed by a king more preoccupied with his pleasure than his
duties, more attentive to his mistresses than his ministers. There
was a strong element of discontent in the land. The radicals of the
1650s did not disappear, nor did the moderate gentry and farmers,
the merchants, clergy and scholars of puritan inclinations who had
supported and serviced the Protectorate. A few of the bolder spirits
were hanged, drawn and quartered, and their limbs put up on the
gates of London to warn of the fate of unsuccessful rebellion. But
armed rebellions continued through the 1660s, while dissenting
ministers and their congregations bore both vocal and silent
witness to the principles which the new government was violating.
Satirical verses circulated clandestinely in manuscript portraying
Charles as a lecher, tyrant and murderer. It was not just the radical
and republican remnants who disapproved of the Restoration
settlement (which was fiercely conservative both politically and
ecclesiastically) but a socially diverse range of protestant Englishmen. Many saw Charles' very public sexual adventuring as offensive to God and an affront to the dignity of the monarchy; nor
could they bring themselves to trust him to preserve the liberties,
property and religion of a protestant nation. They feared that the
absolutist rule essayed by Charles I before the war, and currently
perfected by Louis XIV in France, could be introduced by Charles
II. Even less did they trust Charles' younger brother James, Duke
of York, the heir to the throne, who was a Roman Catholic.

The reign of Charles II was often turbulent and dangerous, never
really secure from the threat of chaos, whether what one feared was
an attempt at absolutism, a radical protestant revolution, a papist
coup, or a foreign invasion. In this climate the mature Dryden
continually reflected upon the problems of government, writing
loyally in support of Charles, but also maintaining a sceptical play
of mind which often saw the comedy of human pretensions. Loyal
but not servile, principled but not inflexible, Dryden spoke to his
age with wit and integrity. He never lost sight of the great
philosophical questions which trouble mankind: his mind was
sceptical and enquiring, but it was also fully informed by the two
languages of the educated seventeenth-century Englishman – the
words of the Bible and the literature of the classical world. We can

trace Dryden's acquisition of these languages through his family and schooling.

*

In some respects the community in which Dryden grew up was culturally stable. The fortunes of his ancestors had risen in the sixteenth century, and by the year 1631 when he was born in the village of Aldwincle in Northamptonshire the Drydens and Pickerings were comfortably established as local landowners. Dryden's family had a strongly puritan ethos, and his grandfather Sir Erasmus Dryden had been the patron of the noted puritan preacher John Dod. Religious commitment entailed political commitment; Sir Erasmus was one of those who refused to pay the forced loan demanded by Charles I, and was consequently imprisoned. Dryden's maternal grandfather, Henry Pickering, was rector of Aldwinckle, while the rector of nearby Titchmarsh, where Dryden's parents settled, was Thomas Hill, a graduate of that Calvinist institution Emmanuel College, Cambridge. Dryden's father, another Erasmus, was a graduate of the same college. It was a stable and godly environment.

And yet this local stability was threatened by the political developments brought about from the centre. The later 1630s were the years of Charles I's personal rule, when he consolidated his autocratic management of the country without a parliament, and encouraged Archbishop Laud in his implementation of high-church doctrine and liturgy. These policies, suggesting a drift towards absolutism and Rome, offered a clear threat to the principles and liberties of families such as the Drydens. Memories of the persecution of protestants under Mary Tudor were kept alive by the great illustrated folio volume of Foxe's *Acts and Monuments*, the 'Book of Martyrs', which was kept in every church. The return of Catholicism would destroy protestant worship and liberty of conscience; it would bring persecution and massacre. But the Drydens learned to live alongside catholic neighbours, for their county was markedly polarised between puritans and recusants.

We know nothing about Dryden's early education, but we can surmise that it would have begun at home, probably with his mother teaching him to read and introducing him to the Bible. The Bible was the word of life, carrying the promise of eternal salvation; it also provided the words for life, the vocabulary and the

conceptual framework through which Dryden understood himself
and his world. It offered a scheme of salvation, the promise that
through the incarnation of God in Christ, and through the sacri-
ficial death of Christ on the cross, man's sin had found and would
find forgiveness. In the Calvinist atmosphere in which Dryden
grew up, this promise was severely modified: according to Calvin
only those who were so elected by God would find eternal
salvation; the rest were predestined to eternal damnation. This
scheme promised the comfort of salvation to the elect, but inflicted
torments of anxiety upon those who were striving to detect within
themselves signs that they were indeed among the saved. However Calvinism impressed Dryden as a boy, in his maturity it had
no attraction for him, and his religious and philosophical thinking
soon took other forms. As well as giving him a personal message of
sin and forgiveness, the Bible provided Dryden with a pattern
through which he could understand history. The intervention of
God in human history made that history significant. Characters
and events before the birth of Christ were read as signs foresha-
dowing the incarnation: such typology made history legible as part
of a divine scheme. And Dryden knew that he was living in the
interval between Christ's death and his second coming. Many
contemporaries thought that the second coming was imminent,
and the language of apocalypse haunts the poetry and pamphlets
of the period. Once again, Dryden's imagination moved away from
these rigid interpretations of history, and embraced other (often
classical and Machiavellian) ways of understanding time and
man's place in the universe. Major poems such as *Absalom and
Achitophel* depend upon this familiarity with a biblical template
which could be laid over contemporary experience, providing a
system of typological interpretation, but they never quite take it
with full and exclusive seriousness; there is always some element
of play which is noticeable when Dryden deploys such schemes.
The words of the Bible nevertheless recur constantly through his
writing, sometimes as obvious allusions, at other times as haunting
half-memories, like the echo of the Book of Job which appears in
his translation of Lucretius.[2] One of the favourite poems of
Dryden's youth was Sylvester's translation of Du Bartas, *The Divine
Weeks and Works*,[3] a poem which celebrates God's creation of the
world. Soon Ovid's *Metamorphoses* would offer other models of
creation.

When he started on his more formal education, probably at a

village school, Dryden would have found that the basis of his study was Latin. Most teachers would still have been using Lily's *A Shorte Introduction of Grammar* (1549), from which a line finds its way into *Absalom and Achitophel*.[4] Children would have been introduced to elementary Latin authors at an early age, so that by the time they arrived at the grammar school they would have a firm grounding in the language. It was Westminster School to which Dryden was sent, the most highly-regarded school of his day. Its headmaster Richard Busby may have acquired a reputation for being over-zealous with the cane, but he ensured that the boys had a thorough training in language and literature. The lower forms had to master Latin and Greek grammar, practising on easy texts including Aesop's fables, Ovid's *De Tristibus* (his laments from exile among the barbarians), the plays of Terence, and the more edifying among the epigrams of Martial. In the third form the boys would read Ovid's *Metamorphoses*, the text which was the poetical handbook of the Renaissance, and one to which Dryden kept returning: he translated large extracts from it for *Examen Poeticum* (1693) and *Fables Ancient and Modern* (1700), as well as making frequent allusions to its tales throughout his writing. Offering stories of the transformation of human beings into animals, trees and stars, it would have stirred any child's mind with a sense of the marvellous. Later it seems also to have appealed to the philosophical bent of the mature Dryden with a sense of the comedy of the human body, the mismatch between body and spirit, and the unstable dividing line between the human and non-human worlds. Fourth formers began the study of Greek from the Westminster anthology, progressing to the Greek New Testament, to Homer and to the rhetorician Isocrates. Though Greek was always of subsidiary interest to Dryden, he maintained his reading knowledge of it, and in old age rediscovered Homer: he translated the last parting of Hector and Andromache from Book VI of the *Iliad* for *Examen Poeticum* and the whole of Book I for his *Fables*; his intention of translating the rest of the poem was frustrated only by illness and death. The Latin satirists Persius and Juvenal were also studied in the higher forms. When publishing his translation from Juvenal and Persius in 1693 Dryden recalled:

I remember I translated this Satyr, when I was a *Kings-Scholar* at *Westminster* School, for a *Thursday* Nights *Exercise*; and believe that it, and many other of my *Exercises* of this nature, in *English*

Verse, are still in the Hands of my *Learned Master*, the Reverend Doctor *Busby*.[5]

The use made of Latin texts was active, consisting of continual analysis, interpretation and translation. The very layout of the pages in Renaissance editions of the classics encouraged the reader to be aware that he must interpret the text actively. The Latin texts were themselves annotated in Latin. On the printed page a passage of Horace would be followed by a prose paraphrase and then a series of explanatory notes. Reading this text would therefore be a matter of constructing 'Horace' from these different elements. Sometimes text and commentary coalesced in the mind, so that we find Dryden adapting part of the commentary by Lubinus when rendering some lines of Juvenal in *Absalom and Achitophel*, and when quoting Latin texts from memory Dryden sometimes inadvertently substitutes a word from the editorial gloss for a word in the text.[6] Glossing, parsing and construing were steps towards a finished translation, which was a major element in the curriculum. The younger boys were set passages of English for translation into Latin prose; later on they might translate a chapter from the Bible into Latin verse. More advanced exercises included turning an episode or speech from an historian into verse, translating an ode by Horace into Greek, or putting it into a different Latin verse-form. These exercises were complemented by the study of rhetorical figures, proverbs and *sententiae*, so that the boys acquired mastery of grammar, idiom and form, and a ready facility in moving between languages. A good style was cultivated: Dryden commented in the Preface to *The Rival Ladies* (1664) that some writers

> constantly close their Lines with Verbs, which though commended sometimes in Writing *Latin*, yet we were Whipt at *Westminster* if we us'd it twice together. (viii 99)

The skill in translating which Dryden acquired at Westminster served him all his life; he also acquired an understanding of the particular characteristics of these several languages. Pondering the nature of English in the Dedication to *Troilus and Cressida* (1679) he writes:

> as our *English* is a composition of the dead and the living

Tongues, there is requir'd a perfect knowledge, not onely of the *Greek* and *Latine*, but of the Old *German*, the *French* and the *Italian*: . . . But how barbarously we yet write and speak . . . I am sufficiently sensible in my own *English*. For I am often put to a stand, in considering whether what I write be the Idiom of the Tongue, or false Grammar, and nonsence couch'd beneath that specious Name of *Anglicisme*; and have no other way to clear my doubts, but by translating my *English* into *Latine*, and thereby trying what sence the words will bear in a more stable language.

(xiii 222)

Dryden's vocabulary and syntax often bear the impress of Latin – not as an affectation but as a way of writing which comes naturally to an educated man of the seventeenth century; nevertheless he is also highly conscious of linguistic relativity, and the instability of the English language. Edmund Waller spoke for many contemporary poets when he wrote:

> Poets that lasting marble seek,
> Must carve in Latin, or in Greek;
> We write in sand, our language grows,
> And, like the tide, our work o'erflows.[7]

Milton wrote Latin poetry, and considered writing *Paradise Lost* in Latin; Dryden has left no Latin compositions at all, and in this respect exemplifies a new confidence in the medium of English. Nevertheless, poets in the reign of Charles II were aware that neither the English language nor its literature had yet achieved European standing, and the anxieties which this produced are visible in the thinly assertive literary criticism of the period, though in his translations (and the accompanying critical essays) where he is matching himself against Horace, Ovid and Virgil we see Dryden developing an assurance of himself and his culture. The continual interplay between English, Hebrew, Roman and Greek cultures which his education fostered seems also to have led Dryden to ponder the relations between different cultures. He was absorbed by the question of whether human nature has always been essentially the same under different historical conditions, a philosophical problem which always impinges upon the translator, particularly when, like Dryden, he uses translation partly as a form of commentary on his own age. All through his career Dryden held the classical, the biblical and the contemporary together, attracted by parallels and amused by mismatches: it became part of his relativistic and sceptical turn of mind.

The experience of Westminster School complicated the inheritance which Dryden had acquired from his family. We have long since abandoned the idea that puritans had cropped hair and sour faces, that their only recreations were smashing stained glass and chopping down maypoles; nevertheless it remains true that puritan attitudes to the pagan classics were divided, and some rejected secular learning altogether. But Dryden's family would not have sent him to Westminster if they had not placed a high value upon a classical education, for in sending him to the capital in the early 1640s at a moment of extraordinary national crisis they were taking a risk with his safety; moreover, they were also taking the risk of entrusting him to a school with a very different political and religious ethos from their own. Busby was no lover of Parliament, and found ways of maintaining his devotion to the Church of England and the monarchy through the Commonwealth period. The schoolboys of Westminster prayed for Charles I on the morning of his execution. Later in 1649 appeared a memorial volume of verses for the young Lord Hastings which stressed his royal connexions and made the book almost an act of covert mourning for the King.[8] Dryden contributed a poem which was extravagant in its conceits and in places outrageously unmetrical, though the disturbed rhythm is no doubt intended as an indication of strong feeling:

> But hasty Winter, with one blast, hath brought
> The hopes of Autumn, Summer, Spring to nought.
> Thus fades the Oak i' th' sprig, i' th' blade the Corn;
> Thus, without Young, this *Phoenix* dies, new born.

> (ll. 77–80)

It is a precocious poem, striving to be modish but succeeding only in looking dated. One might conclude that Dryden had succumbed to Busby's politics, but this poem is too little evidence on which to make such a claim.

*

When Dryden went up to Trinity College, Cambridge in 1650 as a

Westminster scholar he was entering a university which had suffered traumatic changes in the civil war. The purge of the university conducted by the Earl of Manchester on behalf of Parliament in 1644 had resulted in the removal of about half the fellows; forty-nine were ejected from Trinity alone, including the master, Thomas Comber, who had despatched the college's plate to the King to aid the royalist war effort. While the purge removed many recalcitrant opponents of Parliament it did not bring about a uniformity of political or religious opinion among the senior members, nor did it result in any neglect of the traditional academic curriculum. The newly appointed fellows and heads of houses tended to be of puritan stamp, but there is no reason for us to equate puritanism with any lack of concern for academic standards.

The master of Trinity during Dryden's time at the college was Thomas Hill, who had been rector of Dryden's home village of Titchmarsh until 1648. He was intent upon reforming a society which in his eyes had grown slack and even corrupt: it was to be a reformation both godly and academic. Dryden's tutor was John Templer, only some five years older than Dryden himself, and like him a Northamptonshire man. He had come to Trinity from Emmanuel in 1646 to fill one of the fellowships left vacant after the purge. Those writings by Templer which have reached print are all later than the period when he was tutor to Dryden, but they suggest that he was deeply concerned for the peace of church and state, anxious that religion should be heart-felt but not fanatical. Much as he prized inward religion, Templer was aware that the light within us is a fallible guide, and men distort scripture according to their own preferences:

> They speak of a light within them which they own as their guide in this undertaking, and in the mean time neglect the sure word of prophesie. Whereas the scripture sayes to the Law and to the Testimony, they say to their inward light, their understandings being coloured with a false light, they look through it upon the scripture, and so make the scripture appear to them of the same colour; just as to men, that put green or blew glass before their eyes, all the objects round about will appear blew or green.

Templer stresses that reason and revelation are complementary:

Reason and Revelation differ but as a lesser and greater light. The understanding which is the Candle of the Lord, is no more opposite to Revelation, than the Lights, which are known by that name to the Celestial Luminaries with which the Firmament is adorned.[9]

These were subjects (and, indeed, images) which Dryden was to explore for himself in *Religio Laici* (1682) and *The Hind and the Panther* (1687).

The religious temper of Trinity at this time was primarily Calvinist. Its inclinations had always been towards a moderate puritanism, and when the iconoclast Dowsing visited the college he could only manage to bag four cherubim and level the altar steps.[10] Hill's regime seems to have tolerated dissent, though whether this was a willing or a reluctant toleration is impossible to say. He did protect the young Isaac Barrow from the wrath of some fellows after Barrow had made an injudiciously royalist oration on the annual commemoration of 5 November.[11] It may also be a sign of political caution that it was not until 1651 that the arms of the republic replaced those of the King in the hall and the court.[12] On the other hand, Hill once summarily arrested and imprisoned one of the fellows for saying in a tavern that the English parliament were greater rebels than the Irish.[13] Reconstructing the political and religious ethos of the college from this distance is hazardous, particularly when national affairs impinged so directly upon its operation, stirring up passions but at the same time counselling caution in what was said or committed to paper. It is likely that the majority of the fellows conducted college affairs with Trinity's usual mixture of tolerance and malice.

The best guide which we have to the life of an undergraduate at Trinity in the 1650s is the set of rules composed by one of its fellows, Dr James Duport, a distinguished classical scholar.[14] The rules begin by stressing the student's religious duties: to attend chapel every morning and prayers in his tutor's room every evening, to read two or three chapters of the Bible every day, and to read devotional literature, including Herbert's poems. One of his instructions, to 'avoide night-meetings, and Conventicles, in the Courts which are expressly forbidden in the Statutes', raises the interesting possibility that there were illicit religious meetings of dissenting students. Duport gives detailed directions for study:

Use sometimes to translate Greeke into Latine, and Latine into Greeke, for by that meanes, you will the better come to learn the Genius and Idiome of both Tongues.

Make choise of the best Authors in every faculty, as Demosthenes, and Tully [i.e. Cicero], for Oratory, Homer, and Virgil for poetrie, and &c.

Be frequent in exercising your stile, & invention in Greeke Latine, and sometimes in English.

Use your self, (and what if every day) to write some short Epistle, or Essay, or Theame or sometimes verses. Nulla dies sine linea ['no day without a line'].

When you write Latine, let your stile be clear, & perspicuous, smooth, & plaine, & full, not darke, & clowdy, curt, crabbed, & ragged, and let your stile be nervous [i.e. 'sinewy'], & vivid, & masculine, not inert, flat, & languid . . .

In the reading of Authors observe the most remarkable passages, & note them with a black-lead-pen, and reserve them after ward to your Common-place-book . . .

In reading of heathen Poets, especially Juvenal, & Martiall, suck the hony out of the flower, and passe by the weeds.

Much of the curriculum consisted of the study of the major classical texts: history was taught through Greek and Latin historians, philosophy from Aristotle and the scholastic philosophers and theologians of the middle ages and renaissance. The phrasing of Duport's advice suggests a degree of freedom of choice amongst undergraduates as to the texts they were to study, and a concern that their reading should aid their own composition, both in subject matter and style.

As well as maintaining the classical and theological studies which were the primary reason for its existence, Trinity in the seventeenth century also nurtured the new science. But it did so sporadically and sceptically. It was only after the Restoration that the college harboured men whom we might now call 'scientists': Isaac Barrow, the mathematician; John Wilkins, master of the college and one of the founders of the Royal Society; John Ray, the botanist; and Isaac Newton. Even with these men we must be careful when describing them as scientists. That word is a nineteenth-century coinage, and often carries with it nineteenth-century assumptions about science as an instrument of progress and secularisation. Trinity's experimentalists and mathematicians were devout Christians for whom the natural world spoke of God its creator. Barrow resigned the Lucasian chair of mathematics to devote himself fully to theology; his successor, Newton, absorbed himself in the study of the book of Daniel, meditating on the apocalypse and the mysteries of alchemy. In any case, these scientific interests are not in evidence in the 1650s, except in the case of Walter Needham, Dryden's contemporary at Westminster and Trinity, who in 1654 carried out some of the investigations which led to his treatise *De formato foetu* ('on the formation of the foetus') (1667). Scientific studies did not form part of the undergraduate curriculum and are not mentioned by Duport. Only graduates had the freedom to pursue such work, and even then the college did not encourage it, as Newton found. Dryden may have discovered something about the growing interest in experimental science, but it would only have been as a curious sideline. His poetry shows some interest in scientific matters in the early years of the Restoration, and he was elected a fellow of the Royal Society; but he was not sufficiently interested to pay his subscription or attend any meetings, and he was included in the first group of fellows to be expelled.

About Dryden's own experience at Trinity we know little. Indeed, the one fact relating to this period is his punishment by the master and senior fellows, which they recorded on 19 July 1652:

> Agreed then that Dreyden be put out of com[m]ons for a forthnight at least, & that he goe not out of the Colledg during the time aforesaid, excepting to sermons without express leave fro[m] the Master or Vicemaster & that at the end of the forthnight he read a [recantation *deleted*] confession of his crime in the hall at Dinner time; at the three fellowes table.
>
> His crime [alledged *deleted*] was his disobedience to the vicemaster & his contumacy in taking of his punishment inflicted by him.[15]

Discommonsing, walling and public confession were common forms of punishment for undergraduates, but we do not know any details of Dryden's crime. Much later, Thomas Shadwell, venting his anger at Dryden's treatment of him in *Mac Flecknoe*, composed a savage lampoon which includes these allegations:

At *Cambridge* first your scurrilous Vein began
When sawcily you traduc'd a *Nobleman*,
Who for that Crime rebuk'd you on the head,
And you had been Expell'd had you not fled.[16]

We have no means of knowing whether this is an embroidered version of the scrape which Dryden got into in 1652, or another escapade, or simply malicious invention. But we do know that Dryden did not flee Cambridge, nor was he expelled. He graduated in the spring of 1654, third in order of merit amongst the graduates from Trinity, and the college kept his place open for him until midsummer of 1655 in case he wished to return and continue his studies.[17]

*

After leaving Cambridge Dryden found employment as a government servant. In later life his enemies were to make much of his services to Cromwell, and the poem which he wrote in his memory. Here hindsight may be a disadvantage to us. We know that the Republic collapsed within eighteen months of Cromwell's death, but when Dryden became a civil servant a couple of years after the establishment of the Protectorate in 1653, it was a firm, godly, moderate and essentially bourgeois government, secure at home and feared abroad. But if we respect Dryden's service of the Protectorate, can we also respect his adherence to Charles II after the Restoration? As Samuel Johnson wisely observed, 'if he changed, he changed with the nation'.[18] There were of course time-servers, such as the speaker of this ballad:

I am a Turn-coat knave!
Although I do bear it brave,
And do not show all I have;
I can, with tongue and pen, court every sort of men,
And kill 'em as fast agen.
With Zealots I can pray,
With Cavaliers I can play,
With Shop-keepers I can cogg and lye,
And couzen as fast as they. . . .

> But now, I am at Court,
> With men of the better sort,
> And purchase a good report.
> I have the eyes and ears of many brave noble Peers,
>   And slight the poor *Cavileers*.
> Poor knaves! they know not how
> To flatter, cringe, and bow;
>   For he that is wise, and means to rise,
> He must be a *Turn-Coat* too.[19]

Dryden's enemies naturally placed him in this category: Samuel Pordage answered *The Medall* in these lines:

> How easie 'tis to Sail with Wind and Tide?
> Small force will serve upon the stronger side:
> Power serves for Law, the wrong too oft's made right;
> And they are damned, who against power dare fight.
> Wit rides triumphant in Power's Chariot born,
> And deprest Opposites beholds with scorn.
> This well the Author of the *Medal* knew,
> When *Oliver* he for an Hero drew.
> He then Swam with the Tide; appeared a Saint,
> Garnish'd the Devil with Poetick Paint.
> When the Tide turn'd, then strait about he veers,
> And for the stronger side he still appears.
> Then in Heroicks Courts the great, and high,
> And at th' Opprest he lets his Satyrs fly.[20]

These lines turn back upon Dryden the charges of time-serving and opportunism which *The Medall* makes against the Earl of Shaftesbury. It is only in the polarised politics of 1678–82, where adherence to party interests has become a virtue rather than a vice, that the participants' histories are rewritten with such fierce zeal for rectitude. We need not rewrite history with any comparable demand for ideological purity. In any case, Dryden's service of the Protectorate was far from manifesting any radical zeal: in his memorial poem for Cromwell he commemorates the defeat of clamorous factions by a firm ruler, just as he would later in *Absalom and Achitophel*.

Dryden's contact with the Cromwellian establishment came through his cousin Sir Gilbert Pickering, who was the Protector's

Lord Chamberlain. Pickering has gone down in history as a violent and unstable fanatic; John Walker described him as:

> first a presbyterian, then an independent, then a Brownist and afterwards an Anabaptist, he was a most furious, fiery, implacable man; was the principle agent in casting out most of the learned clergy.

But Walker was an enemy, delighting in the defeat of Pickering and his beliefs, and exploiting the victor's privilege of writing history. Pickering certainly knew his own mind, and did not enjoy being crossed. But his parliamentary activities show a firm commitment to a broad, established preaching ministry, and a tolerant attitude to dissent: on a bill for discovering recusants he said that its purpose should be only to secure their obedience to government, for he 'would have no man suffer for his bare opinion'. He also spoke against the barbaric punishment which colleagues wanted to inflict upon the Quaker James Naylor. As for being an enemy to learning, he actually supported the scholarly work on the great Polyglot Bible, whose editors called him 'our great patron', and he served on the committee for establishing a university at Durham.[21] This is the man whom Dryden seems to have served for a while; Shadwell put it like this:

> The next step of Advancement you began,
> Was being Clerk to *Nolls* Lord *Chamberlain*,
> A Sequestrator and Committee-man.
> There all your wholesome Morals you suckt in,
> And got your Gentile Gayety and Meen.
> Your Loyalty you learn'd in *Cromwels* Court.[22]

Despite Shadwell's sarcasm, Cromwell's court was a place of culture, a palace with music, painting and tapestries, albeit neither as extravagant as the court of Charles I nor as licentious as that of his son.

Pickering seems to have passed his young cousin over to John Thurloe, Cromwell's Secretary of State, for on 19 October 1657 Dryden signed a receipt for £50 from Thurloe.[23] We do not know what Dryden had done to earn this sum, for the reward simply comes in a batch of payments made by Thurloe for 'public intelligence'. Perhaps Thurloe liked to recruit young Cambridge

men who were good Latinists and cultured with it, for in 1656
Ralph Cudworth, the master of Christ's College (and no fanatic)
had written to him to recommend several students from Trinity
'that are very good Latinists and well furnisht with all ye Polite
Learning. as Mr. Valentine (a sober discreet man) & Mr Linne (well
known for an excellent Poet)'.[24] Another document reveals that
Dryden became one of the secretaries for French and Latin
tongues, working alongside Milton and Marvell, for they appear
together on the list of officials who were allocated mourning for
Cromwell's funeral procession.[25] One cannot help wondering
whether their work brought the three men together at all closely.
Milton was blind, and in 1655 withdrew from routine office work to
devote himself more to his own studies. But maybe Marvell and
Dryden talked together: they had come from the same college,
though Marvell was ten years older. Perhaps Marvell showed
Dryden a manuscript of his 'An Horatian Ode upon Cromwell's
Return from Ireland': at any rate Dryden knew the poem well
enough to borrow from it in both *Annus Mirabilis* and *Absalom and
Achitophel* before it appeared in print.[26]

Dryden's own first significant poem was prompted by the death
of his employer and ruler, the *Heroique Stanza's, Consecrated to the
Glorious Memory of his most Serene and Renowned Highnesse OLIVER
Late LORD PROTECTOR of this Common-Wealth, &c. Written after the
Celebration of his Funerall*. It opens with a gesture which distances
this poem from the others which have been too hastily produced
by this occasion:

> And now 'tis time; for their Officious haste,
> Who would before have born him to the sky,
> Like *eager Romans* ere all Rites were past
> Did let too soon the *sacred Eagle* fly.
>
> (ll. 1–4)

Dryden did well to reflect carefully before speaking. Cromwell was
a phenomenon without precedent in English history, and the
vocabularies in which a political analysis or a poetic commemoration could be made were not readily available. The execution of
Charles I and the establishment of a republic effected a breach in
the linguistic as well as the political order. Theories of sovereignty

had to be rethought: Milton in *The Tenure of Kings and Magistrates* (1650) argued that rulers are only entrusted with power by the people, who may resume it if their ruler grows tyrannical; Hobbes in *Leviathan* (1651) theorised that in order to escape from the chaos of a lawless state of nature, people transfer their rights to a single absolute sovereign; Winstanley in *The Law of Freedom in a Platform* (1652) developed a programme for a communistic society which would reject the exploitative government of the people by land-owners. The actual government of England was legitimised by continual scrutiny of the Bible and efforts to discover the hand of God at work in the nation's history. Iconographically the seals and coins of the Republic show a curious progression. The seal of the Commonwealth in 1649 showed the House of Commons in session, indicating that it was the sole repository of power and authority; the Protectoral seal for Scotland shows Cromwell on horseback, an imperial image; the coinage of 1658 gives the bust of Cromwell a toga and laurel wreath, and on the reverse the arms are surmounted by a crown.[27] The iconographical problems resulting from the ideological confusion about the status of the new Republic can be seen in Edmund Waller's poem *A Panegyric to my Lord Protector* (1654). He tells his readers that they can take comfort from Cromwell's respectable ancestry: 'One whose extraction from an ancient line/ Gives hope again that well-born men may shine' (ll. 125–6). Waller also employs for Cromwell some traditional Stuart typology: the Plantagenet warrior-kings, the Roman emperor Augustus and the biblical King David are all invoked to authenticate the Protector's rule. Heaven is said to smile upon the conjunction of the greatest leader and the greatest isle.

Dryden's poem shows itself to be well aware of the problem of how to speak about Cromwell: 'our best notes are treason to his fame' and 'in his praise no Arts can liberall be' (ll. 5, 9). In a succession of sober stanzas Dryden analyses Cromwell's character and political skills, celebrates his achievements of peace at home and conquest abroad, and asks how we are to interpret the significance of this figure who has overturned English government. Can we see the hand of divine providence working with him? Cromwell is said to have had innate grandeur, which he 'deriv'd from Heav'n alone,/ For he was great e're Fortune made him so' (ll. 21–2). Unlike some rulers, Cromwell is not the servant of Fortune. In preparing this poem Dryden has evidently been sharpening his sense of practical politics by leafing through

Machiavelli, for stanza 8 adopts an image from chapter 25 of *The Prince*:

> Fortune (that easie Mistresse of the young
> But to her auncient servants coy and hard)
> Him at that age her favorites rank'd among
> When she her best-lov'd *Pompey* did discard.
>
> (ll. 29–32)

Fortune is a mistresse; and it is necessary, to keep her in obedience to ruffle and force her: and we see, that she suffers her self rather to be mastered by those, than by others that proceed coldly. And therefore, as a mistresse, shee is a friend to young men, because they are lesse respective, more rough, and command her with more boldnesse.[28]

Unlike Machiavelli's ruler, Cromwell does not exploit Fortune; he makes no response to her. But he does show political skill in studying the mistakes of others (ll. 33–6) and in weighing up the virtues and weaknesses of his subjects (ll. 97–104). Dryden stresses, however, that he did not seek power:

> And yet *Dominion* was not his Designe,
> We owe that blessing not to him but Heaven,
> Which to faire Acts unsought rewards did joyn,
> Rewards that lesse to him than us were given.
>
> (ll. 37–40)

The rewards were 'unsought': Cromwell is not the Machiavellian prince who aims at dominion, but the just man whose acts are recognised by Heaven. Yet Dryden does not rest content with this analysis; he turns to Cromwell's own nature to look for reasons why he was outstanding. The images which he finds are odd, partly because his poetry still has a residual metaphysical streak, but also because he is unable to invoke the traditional vocabularies, and has instead to hammer out the similes for himself. In stanza 19 we read:

'Tis true, his Count'nance did imprint an awe,
And naturally all souls to his did bow;
As *Wands of Divination* downward draw
And point to Beds where Sov'raign Gold doth grow.

(ll. 73–6)

The gold here (emblematic of sovereignty) is hidden: its presence is only known through the acknowledgement elicited in an almost occult manner from the souls of other men. A similar sense of Cromwell's virtue or true nature being hidden from common measure is found in stanza 32:

Such was our Prince; yet own'd a soul above
The highest Acts it could produce to show:
Thus poor *Mechanique Arts* in publique moove
Whilst the deep Secrets beyond practice goe.

(ll. 125–8)

'Practice' here means both 'performance' and 'calculation'. The platonic undertones of this concept are more apparent in stanza 26:

Or he their single vertues did survay
By *intuition* in his own large brest,
Where all the rich *Idea's* of them lay,
That were the rule and measure to the rest.

(ll. 101–4)

So in Cromwell's soul are lodged the platonic Ideas of those virtues which are dispersed in others.

Dryden is revising here the neo-platonism which twenty years earlier had bolstered the complacency of the Caroline court in poems and masques, but this is now an *ad hominem* platonism. James and Charles sat at the focal point of masques which fabricated a universal harmony, but no great platonic system endorses Cromwell. His innate ability and virtue naturally compel recognition. Yet the neo-platonism which Dryden adapts into this reduced, more sober form is but one of the inherited images which he uses. Cromwell is credited with the perfect, circular wholeness which Jonson extolled in his cavalier Sons (l. 18); his palms – unlike those of Charles I in the frontispiece to *Eikon Basilike* – flourish without weights (ll. 57–8); and the halcyons which for cavalier poets had graced the peace of the early Stuarts nest again to confer serenity on the Protector and his legacy (l. 144). The halcyons, however, also remind us that the Pax Cromwelliana may be short lived. The birds were supposed to nest at sea around the time of the winter solstice, when storms subsided for a fortnight and provided halcyon days of calm. But this can only be an interval, and if one recognises this dimension to the image, the caution of the poem's ending becomes more striking:

> No Civill broyles have since his death arose,
> But *Faction* now by *Habit* does obey:
> And *Warrs* have that respect for his repose,
> As *Winds* for *Halcyons* when they breed at Sea.
>
> His Ashes in a peacefull Urne shall rest,
> His Name a great example stands to show
> How strangely high endeavours may be blest,
> Where *Piety* and *valour* joyntly goe.

(ll. 141–8)

Dryden's silence on the future of the Protectorate is eloquent.

2
The New Writer
1660–7

We almost lose sight of Dryden between the death of Cromwell in September 1658 and the restoration of the monarchy in May 1660. Galling though it is to have to depend upon such a source, Shadwell's *The Medal of John Bayes* (1682) provides some necessary clues:

> [Cromwell] being dead, who should the slave prefer,
> He turn'd a Journey-man t'a Bookseller;
> Writ Prefaces to Books for Meat and Drink,
> And as he paid, he would both write and think.
> Then by th' assistance of a Noble *Knight*
> Th' hadst plenty, ease, and liberty to write.

(pp. 8–9)

Shadwell's footnotes identify the bookseller as '*Mr*. Herringman, *who kept him in his House for that purpose*', and the knight as '*Sir* R.H. *who kept him generously at his own House.*' It is indeed possible that Dryden wrote several prefaces to books which Herringman published, though this can hardly have provided him with a very lucrative living. The knight with whom Dryden subsequently lodged was Sir Robert Howard, son of the Earl of Berkshire and brother of Elizabeth, whom Dryden was to marry in 1663. The Howard-Dryden alliance makes a convenient illustration of the complexities of allegiances in the early Restoration. The Howard family was England's premier catholic clan, and although the Berkshire branch of it was protestant, there is some reason to believe that Lady Elizabeth was a catholic.[1] The old Earl had been a loyal supporter of Charles I, but his loyalty received little reward from Charles II, and his finances were precarious. Dryden as an ex-Commonwealthsman may seem an unlikely son-in-law for the Earl, but to the Howards Dryden may have appeared a talented

21

young man likely to make his mark, while to Dryden an aristocratic alliance had social and political advantages. Of the personal feelings between Dryden and Elizabeth we know nothing.

Though Shadwell's lines are jaundiced, they do remind us that it was a matter of some urgency for Dryden to find a secure means of earning his living: he was nearing thirty, his past service in government was no recommendation, he was without access to the circles of power, and as yet had no literary reputation. He now sought to establish himself in the world of letters through a series of poems addressed to some of the leading figures of the age.

Dryden began with a poem to Robert Howard, prefixed to Howard's collection called *Poems* (1660). The poem is a meditation on the nature of art, and the place which English poetry can take in the new order. He starts by praising Howard for the ease of his writing:

> As there is Musick uninform'd by Art
> In those wild Notes, which with a merry heart
> The Birds in unfrequented shades expresse,
> Who better taught at home, yet please us lesse:
> So in your Verse, a native sweetnesse dwells,
> Which shames Composure, and its Art excells.

(ll. 1–6)

Howard's poetry does not exhibit the stress of laboured composition ('Composure'), but comes naturally, so either 'your Art hides Art', according to the classical precept *ars est celare artem* ('the art lies in concealing the art'), or Howard's muse has some special grace, or Fortune has aided the composition. This is not merely a compliment to Howard's skill, but an exploration of the dynamics of creativity. Observers find it hard to see 'What hidden springs within the Engine be' (l. 22), which implies that there may be a physiological mechanism there if only science could discover it. Alternatively:

> is it Fortune's work, that in your head
> The curious Net that is for fancies spread,
> Let's through its Meshes every meaner thought,
> While rich Idea's there are onely caught?

(ll. 25–8)

But the idea of art being produced by the capricious power of
Fortune is rejected:

> this is a piece too fair
> To be the child of Chance, and not of Care.
> No Atoms casually together hurl'd
> Could e're produce so beautifull a world.

>   (ll. 29–32)

These passages show an interest in epistemology. Dryden is
exploring the question of how we know and, in physiological
terms, how we think. Human science and artistry may be on the
threshold of a new era, but the idea that the world is ultimately
chaotic, and not amenable to human knowledge, cannot be dismissed altogether: the topic may be gracefully dismissed here, but it
will recur.[2]

To S*ʳ Robert Howard* also considers the art of translation. Howard's collection includes some versions of Virgil and Statius, and
Dryden comments on Howard's rendering of *Aeneid* IV:

> your Art the way has found
> To make improvement of the richest ground,
> That soil which those immortall Lawrells bore,
> That once the sacred *Maro*'s [Virgil's] temples wore.

>   (ll. 55–8)

If the hyperbole here moves uncomfortably close to satire,[3] the
lines nevertheless include the important idea that one of the tasks
of Restoration poetry will be to 'make improvement of the richest
ground'. Albeit in a very preliminary way, Dryden is marking out
the ground for the new English poetry in general, and for his own
poetry and criticism in particular.

Finally, Dryden's poem pays tribute to Howard's political presci-
ence, for 'Ere our weak eyes discern'd the doubtfull streak/ Of
light, you saw great *Charls* his morning break.' (ll. 89–90). This
compliment to Howard's sense of timing in publishing his poems
on the eve of the Restoration raises the problem of the function of
public poetry in this period. When reading the poems which
Dryden addressed to various public figures in the early 1660s, we
should recall that panegyric poetry had a didactic role.[4] This idea

has a long ancestry. The Roman poets who addressed their rulers often managed to include critical or admonitory material, and Restoration writers who had studied Augustan literature knew that Virgil, Horace and Ovid were not uncritical supporters of Augustus. Panegyric classically seeks to voice national matters which transcend parties and personalities, and to delineate humanistic moral values. Its praise of a public figure is a description of the virtues which such a person ought to have, and as Erasmus said, praise undeserved automatically becomes satire. Much Restoration panegyric is merely servile and opportunistic, but Dryden's early public poetry presses beyond the individuals whom it addresses to the larger causes which they represent, and in so doing it takes part in the urgent process of national self-definition which was so prominent in the culture of the 1660s.

*

Dryden's poem on the Restoration, *Astraea Redux* (1660), shows itself to be conscious of the problem of honest public speech, and in particular of the linguistic problem which now confronts writers. Astraea was the goddess of justice who according to Roman mythology left the earth in despair at human wickedness; now with the restoration of the monarchy justice too is brought back (*redux*). The allusion is Virgilian (*Eclogue* iv 6) and is supported by a suggestion that Charles is a second Aeneas refounding Troy after years of tribulation (ll. 120–4) – though Dryden tactfully says nothing about any Dido. These are among the gestures through which the poem – like many of its rivals for Charles' attention – associates the King with the Emperor Augustus. Both had brought peace and stability to their countries after years of civil war. *Astraea Redux* claims that the English Augustus is inaugurating a new period of time in which the arts both of peace and war will flourish:

> Oh Happy Age! Oh times like those alone
> By Fate reserv'd for Great *Augustus* Throne!
> When the joint growth of Armes and Arts foreshew
> The World a Monarch, and that Monarch *You*.

(ll. 320–3)

But this is only offered as a culminating image after the poem has explored the practical politics of Charles' restoration. The Interregnum is presented as a period of anarchy:

> For when by their designing Leaders taught
> To strike at Pow'r which for themselves they sought,
> The Vulgar gull'd into Rebellion, arm'd,
> Their blood to action by the Prize was warm'd . . .
> The Rabble now such Freedom did enjoy,
> As Winds at Sea that use it to destroy:
> Blind as the *Cyclops*, and as wild as he,
> They own'd a lawless salvage Libertie,
> Like that our painted Ancestours so priz'd
> Ere Empires Arts their Breasts had Civiliz'd.

> > (ll. 31–4; 43–8)

The rabble have been exploited by their politically skilful leaders, and the pursuit of power by unscrupulous individuals has led the nation back into the primitive uncivilised state which existed before the arrival of the Romans with their arts of empire. The emphasis here on the 'designing Leaders' of the Parliamentarian cause may derive from Dryden's own observations in the late 1650s, but it also forms part of the poem's interest in the mechanics of politics. Dryden considers how the Restoration was actually effected; it was General George Monck who played the crucial role:

> 'Twas *MONCK* whom Providence design'd to loose
> Those real bonds false freedom did impose.
> The blessed Saints that watch'd this turning Scene
> Did from their Stars with joyful wonder leane,
> To see small clues [threads] draw vastest weights along,
> Not in their bulk but in their order strong.

> > (ll. 151–6)

Providence does not intervene by upsetting the normal course of events, but works through it, having Monck achieve great results from small actions like a series of pulleys moving a huge weight. This chain of cause and effect is perceptible to the saints (who are looking at a kind of stage play) but not to us, and *Astraea Redux* is aware that the images which we contrive to explain things may be misleading:

> With ease such fond *Chymaera's* we pursue
> As fancy frames for fancy to subdue,
> But when our selves to action we betake
> It shuns the Mint like gold that Chymists make:

(ll. 159–62)

By implication, not only the politician but the poet too must allow his easy designs to be tested against reality. Dryden does just that, for the poem acknowledges that the deployment of Augustan and providential language is a rhetorical gesture designed not only to explain but to persuade.

In analysing the role of Monck, Dryden takes the traditional image of the body politic and reworks it in the light of his physiological knowledge:

> How hard was then his task, at once to be
> What in the body natural we see
> Mans Architect distinctly did ordain
> The charge of Muscles, Nerves, and of the Brain;
> Through viewless Conduits Spirits to dispense,
> The Springs of Motion from the Seat of Sense.

(ll. 163–8)

Monck had to carry out in the state those functions which in the body God designated separately to the brain which conceives ideas, the nerves which transmit them, and the muscles which execute them. Moreover, all this happens unseen, it is 'viewless', and (like Cromwell) Monck acts without outside observers perceiving the connexion between the events and their designer. The onlookers see the effects but not the cause, nor can we see the individual stages of the process:

> Yet as wise Artists mix their colours so
> That by degrees they from each other go,
> Black steals unheeded from the neighb'ring white
> Without offending the well cous'ned sight:
> So on us stole our blessed change; while we
> Th' effect did feel but scarce the manner see.

(ll. 125–30)

But the artistic effect which the poem offers us is more easily seen; indeed, *Astraea Redux* seems to be calling attention to the difficulty which art has in finding appropriate words for the real world of events. The conceits are palpable:

> [Charles] found his life too true a Pilgrimage.

> (l. 54)

> It is no longer Motion cheats your view,
> As you meet it, the Land approacheth you.

> (ll. 252–3)

The explanations of art are self-consciously shown to be fictions.

This self-consciousness extends to the poem's naming of the King. The *Heroique Stanza's* had tackled the problematic status and title of Cromwell. That poem offered praise 'to his name' (l. 7); he was 'pres'd down by his own weighty name' (l. 135); after his death 'His Name a great example stands' (l. 146). But Cromwell's own status and nomenclature were as awkward as that of the Commonwealth itself, for he declined the name of king while exercising kingly power and using royal iconography. *Astraea Redux* is also concerned with names. Astraea, Jove, Charles I, Piso, David, Adam, Aeneas, Moses and Augustus are all tried out as possible names for Charles II. His grandfather Henri IV gained the 'name of *Great*',

> Who yet a king alone in Name and Right,
> With hunger, cold and angry *Jove* did fight;

> (ll. 99–100)

This antithesis between shadow and substance applies also to religion during the Interregnum, when

> Religions name against it self was made;
> The shadow serv'd the substance to invade:

> (ll. 191–2)

The ships which carry the royal family from Holland have been renamed, so that

> The *Naseby* now no longer *Englands* shame
> But better to be lost in *Charles* his name . . .
> Receives her Lord:

> (ll. 230–3)

Such renaming reverses the revolution of the 1640s and 1650s which had involved many instances of public renaming as new leaders assumed control of the language of government, and radical groups produced new vocabularies for the description of English history and society. On a formal philosophical level Hobbes' *Leviathan* (1651) propounded a nominalism which embraced all areas of life, whereby the 'words of Good, Evill and Contemptible, are ever used with relation to the person that useth them: There being nothing simply and absolutely so'.[5] These developments, along with the upheavals in the systems of law and religion which had previously served to authenticate kingship, had made the language of authority deeply problematic, and the Restoration could not obliterate the trauma which these interlocking codes had undergone. Charles I, the ruler of what his poets had called the new Troy, had suffered the same fate as King Priam; he too had become 'a headless carcass, and a nameless thing'.[6] *Astraea Redux* gains strength and honesty from its recognition that public speech blunders into the unknowable, and its admission that knowing and naming are crucial issues for the new Restoration culture.

*

Dryden's subsequent poems on the Restoration settlement are less thoughtful achievements. *To His Sacred Majesty, A Panegyrick on his Coronation* (1661) begins by likening the Restoration to the emergence of Noah's ark after the flood, 'when that flood in its own depths was drowned' (l. 5), which in suggesting that the Commonwealth defeated itself, neatly combines an accurate political observation with an intimation of providential approval. The account of the coronation repeatedly points to the limitations of the poet's ability to find a suitable language, for many of the images are reflexive: the strains of music 'lye like Bees in their own sweetnesse drowned' (l. 56); the church which is to sanctify Charles is less holy than the king himself (ll. 45–6); he himself is the greatest part of the entertainment which is held in his honour (l. 34). This acknowledgement of inadequacy recurs in the poem *To My Lord Chancellor, Presented on New-years-day* (1662), where it becomes an extravagant compliment:

> In open prospect nothing bounds our eye
> Until the Earth seems joyn'd unto the Sky:
> So in this Hemisphaer our utmost view
> Is only bounded by our King and you:
> Our sight is limited where you are joyn'd
> And beyond that no farther Heav'n can find.
>
>   (ll. 31–6)

Dryden then tries out an ungainly neo-platonic conceit to describe the relationship between Charles and his Chancellor, the Earl of Clarendon:

> So well your Vertues do with his agree
> That though your Orbs of different greatness be,
> Yet both are for each others use dispos'd,
> His to inclose, and yours to be inclos'd.
>
>   (ll. 37–40)

Thinking again about how rulers operate, Dryden says that Clarendon works

> by means as noble as your end:
> Which, should you veil, we might unwind the clue
> As men do Nature, till we came to you.
>
>   (ll. 70–2)

Nevertheless, the onlooker cannot fully read the Chancellor:

> Such is the mighty swiftnesse of your mind
> That (like the earth's) it leaves our sence behind;
> While you so smoothly turn and roul our Sphear,
> That rapid motion does but rest appear.
> For as in Natures swiftnesse, with the throng

> Of flying Orbs while ours is born along,
> All seems at rest to the deluded eye . . .
> We rest in Peace and yet in motion share.

> (ll. 109–18)

The perception of the observer is limited by his own position, and he is involved in (and a beneficiary of) the activity which he attempts to understand. The scientific images remind us that Dryden's poetry is still engaging with the problems of knowledge and perception, even though there is on this occasion little more than flattery in the idea.

The notion that the new Restoration culture makes new kinds of intellectual enquiry both possible and necessary finds more extended expression in Dryden's poem *To my Honour'd Friend, D*ʳ *Charleton, on his learned and useful Works*. Walter Charleton was the friend who in 1662 proposed Dryden for membership of the Royal Society, and this poem prefaces Charleton's book *Chorea Gigantum* (1663) on the origins of Stonehenge. Man is emerging from tyranny, this time not political servitude but the enslavement of free-born reason to Aristotle, a period of idolatrous homage 'to a *Name*' (l. 15). Men had been gulled into buying 'Emp'rique Wares, or Charms,/ Hard Words seal'd up with *Aristotle*'s Armes' (ll. 7–8). Now men put less trust in names, in inherited formulae and folk remedies which work without people knowing why (the meaning of 'empiric' here); Restoration Englishmen have begun to find out for themselves how things work:

> Among th' *Assertors* of free Reason's claim,
> Th' *English* are not the least in Worth, or Fame.
> The World to *Bacon* does not onely owe
> Its *present* Knowledge, but its *future* too.

> (ll. 21–4)

Bacon has laid the foundations of knowledge, and other Englishmen in various scientific fields have built on it: Gilbert, Boyle, Harvey and Ent. The poem ends with a graceful gesture which asserts the importance of the Restoration of the monarchy as a restoration of English culture. Stonehenge in Charleton's view had been a druidic temple; it was also the place where Charles had

rested when escaping from his pursuers after the battle of
Worcester:

> His *Refuge* then was for a *Temple* shown:
> But, *He* Restor'd, 'tis now become a *Throne*.

(ll. 57–8)

It would be easy to dismiss as gauche or merely opportunist the
claims which Dryden's poems from the early 1660s make for the
new order, but we should suspend our cynicism. There was a
genuinely new confidence and excitement at work in several
cultural fields, as the founding of the Royal Society in 1662
indicates. These early poems both praise and probe. Dryden is
contemplating the mechanics of political activity, and at the same
time beginning to reflect epistemologically upon the processes of
knowledge and the forms through which our knowledge is medi-
ated.

*

Dryden's first major poem manages to combine celebration and
scepticism in a more searching way. *Annus Mirabilis: The Year of
Wonders, 1666* (1667) was composed in the closing months of the
year which had seen the Second Dutch War and the Fire of
London. It had been expected to be a year of wonders because
'1666' combines the millenium with the number of the Beast from
the book of Revelation. Critics of the Restoration establishment
foretold a year of disaster as divine retribution for the immoral and
ungodly behaviour of the court, while those like the astrologer
William Lilly who were more sympathetic to the King predicted a
year of triumph for Charles and of confusion to his enemies. After
the event both anglican and nonconformist preachers pronounced
the fire to be the judgment of God. Opinion as to the success of the
naval actions was divided, but many regarded them as humiliat-
ing, and several satires on the conduct of the war circulated in
manuscript. Samuel Pepys was among those outraged by the
incompetence evident in the handling of events at sea, and
contemplated trying his own hand at a satire.[7] *Annus Mirabilis* is
thus addressing itself to events which had already been interpreted, and it engages with the problems of interpretation. The
poem does praise the Stuart leadership, but not naively: it is

dedicated to the City of London, whose relations with the monarchy were often strained, and it carries a preface to Sir Robert Howard, by now a parliamentarian whose loyalty to court interests was by no means clear. Moreover, while the poem does make some exaggerated gestures in praise of the Stuarts, and discreetly covers over some embarrassing incidents, its general tendency is to invite us to look at the events of 1666 with a probing, radical vision. Though beginning as if it will be blithely propagandist, the poem actually becomes deep and complex as it wrestles with the problems of understanding and representation.

The poem's epigraphs draw our attention to two ways of thinking about events. The first is a quotation from Trajan's letter to Pliny: *Multum interest res poscat, an homines latius imperare velint* (the validity of a course of action 'depends very much on whether the occasion demands it, or whether men are just eager to extend their power more widely'). This invites the reader to weigh up the morality of public actions, and to recall that most wars are prompted by mere expediency and desire for gain. The second epigraph is from Virgil: *Urbs antiqua ruit, multos dominata per annos* ('the ancient city, which had ruled for many years, is falling'). This associates London with Troy, deploying the mythological association of Restoration with Roman culture. In a sense the two epigraphs stand for the two kinds of interpretation between which the poem plays, the mythologising and the sceptical. The opening stanzas present the causes of the war with Holland from a point of view which is both chauvinistic and politically astute. In saying that 'Trade, which like bloud should circularly flow,/ Stop'd in their Channels, found its freedom lost' (ll. 5–6), Dryden deftly images the commercial rivalry which prompted the war. He depicts Louis XIV as a Machiavellian prince who had 'vast designs' (l. 28) which are pursued through dissimulation and false friendship:

> See how he feeds th' *Iberian* with delays,
> To render us his timely friendship vain;
> And, while his secret Soul on *Flanders* preys,
> He rocks the Cradle of the Babe of *Spain*.

> (ll. 29–32)

By contrast Charles II is not a scheming politician but a thoughtful king:

> This saw our King; and long within his breast
> His pensive counsels ballanc'd too and fro;

(ll. 37–8)

The presentation of the English cause does put Charles in a good light, and also passes over some awkward episodes in silence, such as the scandalous behaviour of Henry Brounker, secretary to the Duke of York, who fabricated an order from his master to slacken sail because he was tired of pursuing the Dutch. But since Dryden was composing *Annus Mirabilis* at his father-in-law's house in Wiltshire, where he and Elizabeth had gone to avoid the plague, he was dependent upon such written accounts as happened to reach him, chiefly government newsbooks. Even Samuel Pepys, who stayed in London and had a professional interest in the naval war, had only a hazy and tardy impression of what happened, and was often a prey to rumour. If we place *Annus Mirabilis* alongside the official reports which Dryden would have read, it becomes apparent that he followed their descriptions closely for the factual portions of the poem,[8] and shared something of their religious awareness, but he did not allow his interpretation of events to be simply partisan.

The political thinking in *Annus Mirabilis* is couched partly in classical terms, through the extended use of Roman parallels. It is indicative of the mode of *Annus Mirabilis* that no one parallel predominates, for Dryden does not allow his reader to imagine that Restoration England can be read through any simple parallel with a single period of Roman history, such as the age of Augustus. The first classical parallel which we meet is in fact with republican Rome and its wars with Carthage:

> Thus mighty in her Ships, stood *Carthage* long,
> And swept the riches of the world from far;
> Yet stoop'd to *Rome*, less wealthy, but more strong:
> And this may prove our second Punick War.

(ll. 17–20)

This admits the practicalities of power, that Rome depends on its strength, but the stanza is also proleptic: 'this *may* prove' urges the comparison but realises that the poem has no power to make it true. That power resides only with its readers. Dryden's Roman allusions also speak of a people who have learned how to endure defeat, and how to turn defeat into victory. Albemarle's calm defiance of the foes who encircle him compels admiration comparable with the wonder of the Gauls who entered Rome to find the elders sitting motionless in their chairs awaiting death (ll. 249–52). Reading the Latin historians in his schooldays would have accustomed Dryden to the idea that Rome achieved greatness by knowing how to bring victory out of defeat, for the epitome of Roman history by Lucius Florus (the basic text book for beginners) is a catalogue of the wars which made Rome a nation, with the moments of triumph and disaster made especially prominent; as Florus says, 'By so many toils and dangers have they been buffeted that Valour and Fortune seem to have competed to establish the Roman empire' (l. Intro. 2).

What sustained the Romans was not simple bravery but reverence for the gods, the city and the family, a feeling which was called *pietas*. Virgil's recurring epithet for Aeneas, *pius* ('dutiful'), is used by Dryden several times in its English version with the Latin connotations. The commanders who shield Albemarle from his enemies stretch out their 'pious wings' (l. 255); Prince Rupert seeks to aid his comrades with the 'pious care' of an eagle for its young (l. 425); the City of London's present of a ship to the King is 'piously design'd' (l. 613), and Charles himself sheds 'pious tears' for his people (l. 958). Like Augustus, Charles is also *Pater Patriae*, 'The Father of the people' (l. 1141). This traditional metaphor does not imply a paternalistic attitude in the modern sense, for the bond between ruler and people is reciprocal, and the generous exercise of one's role brings rewards:

> The doubled charge his Subjects love supplies,
> Who, in that bounty, to themselves are kind:
> So glad *Egyptians* see their *Nilus* rise,
> And in his plenty their abundance find.

(ll. 181–4)

> This Royal bounty brought its own reward,
> And, in their minds, so deep did print the sense . . .

(ll. 1145–6)

The image of the Nile suggests that such a relation between subjects and ruler is not only mutually enriching, but part of the natural order.

Of all the classical influences upon *Annus Mirabilis* the most important is that of Virgil, as Dryden himself acknowledges in his prefatory *Account of the ensuing Poem*. Yet Virgil offers no direct model for such a poem: formally, *Annus Mirabilis* owes nothing to the epic. Dryden describes it instead as 'An Historical Poem'; it is concerned with the events of one year, and chronological coincidence will not of itself create a quasi-epic unity from events as causally diverse as the fire and the war. Rather, *Annus Mirabilis* is historical in that it attends to the events of history as they are experienced, and it is therefore quite removed from that understanding of the epic which was shortly to be formulated by Le Bossu, who looked for a unity of design which would express a single and coherent moral message.[9] *Annus Mirabilis* is designedly incapable of that kind of coherence because it is attempting to understand events as they happen, aware of the awkward discrepancies which arise between our experience and the interpretations which we would like to make of it.

The *Account* discusses the different poetic manners of Ovid and Virgil, and it may be that these two writers offered Dryden rival, and equally necessary mythologies. Virgil is the poet of stability and culture. His *Georgics* speak of how man cultivates the earth, managing its resources and acting in conformity with natural laws so as to achieve the best return for his labour. Man is clearly distinct from the natural world, and the *Georgics* show him how to maintain that separation and mastery. The *Aeneid* tells of an escape from the burning ruins of one civilisation and the founding of another; the characters emerge from the chaos of flames and the pathless wilderness of the sea to found a city and mark out its boundaries. The threat of dissolution and anarchy is overcome by culture and civilisation, the marking out of human territory. Ovid, however, is the poet of changes and transformation, through which man loses his human form and becomes a beast or plant or inanimate object. Ovid shows us the mental chaos which results when passion breaks down the ordered forms of reason; he describes states in which all distinctions are lost. He is the poet of mixture, of incestuous passion, and of miscegenation between gods and men where the boundaries of taboo are crossed. The dividing lines which separate man from the non-human world are blurred, and his separate identity is lost. It is indicative of the honesty and complexity of *Annus Mirabilis* that Dryden should have been influenced not only by the ordering capacity of Virgil but also by the Ovidian perception of life's tendency to dissolve into confusion. Dryden's poem tries not to impose an artificial pattern on the experience which it relates, and includes a recognition of where the organising faculties of political policy and poetic structure break down. The two philosophies are expressed in two different kinds of art, and while expressing a preference for Virgil, Dryden conceded much to the example of Ovid. Nature is in disorder, but it must be comprehended, and so we watch the struggle of a mind to be at once understanding, and honest to life's capacity to defeat understanding.

Dryden shares Virgil's concern with how man should relate to nature and the gods if he is to achieve a happy life. In one of Dryden's adaptations from the *Georgics* we glimpse his intuition of a divine economy: Charles

> . . . first, survey'd the charge with careful eyes,
>   Which none but mighty Monarchs could maintain;
> Yet judg'd, like vapours that from Limbecks rise,
>   It would in richer showers descend again.

(ll. 49–52)

In government, chemistry and agriculture the same pattern is to be found, but the reciprocity in this natural economy operates only if man himself works in harmony with earth and heaven. Art works on nature to create the material advantages of life, as Dryden recalls when depicting the origin of shipping (ll. 621–4). The state itself, created and organised by art, is likewise in harmony with nature:

> All hands employ'd, the Royal work grows warm,
>   Like labouring Bees on a long Summers day,
> Some sound the Trumpet for the rest to swarm,
>   And some on bells of tasted Lillies play:
>
> With glewy wax some new foundation lay
>   Of Virgin combs, which from the roof are hung:

> Some arm'd within doors, upon duty stay,
>   Or tend the sick, or educate the young.

                    (ll. 573–80)

There are perhaps two ways of reading the politics of this image. We might stress its capacity to naturalise the state, to place it safely within the natural order as something which is beyond criticism; alternatively we might stress its presentation of the state as something which is constructed and therefore may be reconstructed. It seems characteristic of this poem that both the mythologising and the demythologising impulses are present.

This image is one of many drawn from nature in *Annus Mirabilis*. They range from a cornfield blasted by a thunderstorm (ll. 445–8) to larks scared of the hawk (l. 780), a spider waiting for its prey (ll. 717–20), and the frozen ground thawing to produce spring shoots (ll. 1133–6). Few of these would have surprised Virgil, but Dryden ranges beyond inherited examples. When he writes that Albemarle's 'eclips'd estate . . . like the Sun's, more wonders does afford' (ll. 359–60) he writes as one who would have seen an eclipse of the sun on 22 June 1666 and read observations of it in the transactions of the Royal Society. He often writes as a direct observer of nature, as when Albemarle is surrounded by the Dutch:

> Have you not seen when, whistled from the fist,
>   Some Falcon stoops at what her eye design'd,
> And, with her eagerness, the quarry miss'd,
>   Straight flies at check, and clips it down the wind,
>
> The dastard Crow, that to the wood made wing,
>   And sees the Groves no shelter can afford,
> With her loud Kaws her Craven kind does bring,
>   Who, safe in numbers cuff the noble Bird?

                    (ll. 341–8)

The vocabulary has a countryman's accuracy: 'whistled from', 'stoops', 'at check' and 'clips it' are all technical terms in falconry. One of Dryden's achievements in *Annus Mirabilis* is to refine our apprehension of how close civilised man is to animal and inanimate nature.

Some of the natural images are influenced by Ovid. The most moving of all is the simile of the hare chased by a dog, which is taken from the first book of the *Metamorphoses*:

> So have I seen some fearful Hare maintain
> A Course, till tir'd before the Dog she lay:
> Who, stretch'd behind her, pants upon the plain,
> Past pow'r to kill as she to get away.
>
> With his loll'd tongue he faintly licks his prey,
> His warm breath blows her flix up as she lies:
> She, trembling, creeps upon the ground away,
> And looks back to him with beseeching eyes.
>
> (ll. 521–8)

'So have I seen', begins Dryden, speaking in his own voice to encourage our perception. He omits Ovid's witty turn *hic praedam pedibus petit, ille salutem* ('he seeks his prey on flying feet, but she [seeks] safety') which with its obvious alliteration draws attention to its own cleverness. Ovid offers the excitement of the chase, *iam iamque tenere/ sperat*, ('now, now he hopes he has her') while Dryden draws attention to the animals' exhaustion. In Ovid the hare barely escapes from the teeth of the dog: *ipsis/ morsibus eripitur tangentiaque ora relinquit* ('she barely escapes from those fangs, and leaves behind the jaws just closing on her'); in Dryden the dog 'faintly licks' his prey in weariness. Dryden modifies Ovid's wit to reveal the poignancy of the encounter. This reworking of Ovid illustrates two forms of scepticism which seem characteristic of this poem. First, the poem questions the mythologies of heroic conquest and imperial glory, which is achieved here by the introduction into a battle scene of these images of exhaustion, pain and defeat among ordinary animals; secondly, the poem encourages us to cross the normally secure boundaries between the human and the animal by the attribution of recognisably human feelings to these creatures.

An Ovidian wit sometimes creeps into the religious explanations which the poem offers when it invokes divine providence. When the poem claims that the storms which robbed the English ships of their prey relent and restore some of them as prizes, nature seems

to exhibit a kind of divine economy (ll. 117–24), but the witty shape
to the observation makes it hard to read this as a straight example
of divine providence. In the case of the Fire of London, Dryden
would have read in *The London Gazette* that the flames were
providentially diverted from the naval magazines, whose loss
would have left the country virtually defenceless:

> And we have further this infinite cause particularly to give God
> thanks that the fire did not happen in any of those places where
> his Majesties Naval stores are kept, so as tho it hath pleased God
> to visit with his own hand, he hath not, by disfurnishing us with
> the means of carrying on the War, subjected us to our enemies.[10]

But the acknowledgement of divine intervention in *Annus Mirabilis*
is made through an extravagantly witty image which almost
subverts the point which it is making. God prepares to extinguish
the flames:

> An hollow chrystal Pyramid he takes,
> In firmamental waters dipt above;
> Of it a brode Extinguisher he makes,
> And hoods the flames that to their quarry strove.

> (ll. 1121–4)

Contemporaries ridiculed this and similar images, and one reader
composed a parody on the endpaper of his copy:

> An Hollow far-fetcht Metaphor he takes
> In non-sense dipt of his fantastick braine
> Of which a broad extinguisher he makes
> Which hoods his witt & stifles all his flame.[11]

The strangeness of some of Dryden's images could be attributed to
the embarrassment which he faced in continuing to be a kind of
metaphysical poet in a different philosophical climate, but we must
also recognise that Dryden actively enjoyed the comic disparity
between physical and spiritual, and the mis-match of these two
elements in man.[12] This image and many like it are deliberately
odd, made so in order to draw our attention to the puzzlement of
language when called upon to express superhuman matters. The

wit is by its very quirkiness pointing up the comedy inherent in man's attempt to understand the universe, and in so doing is theologically quite orthodox.

Nevertheless, the exotic images of divine providence at work in events are made to coexist with more sober and forceful classical philosophies. The most striking instance is the set of stanzas adapted from Petronius' *Satyricon*. The lines tell of the sailor whose return is longed for by his family:

> This carefull Husband had been long away,
>   Whom his chast wife and little children mourn;
> Who on their fingers learn'd to tell the day
>   On which their Father promis'd to return.
>
> Such are the proud designs of human kind,
>   And so we suffer Shipwrack every where!
> Alas, what Port can such a Pilot find,
>   Who in the night of Fate must blindly steer!
>
> (ll. 133–40)

Though based on Petronius, the most eloquent parts are Dryden's own: the detail of the children counting the days on their fingers, and the image of man steering blindly through the night of fate. Christian teaching about the providence of God is put aside as Dryden gives serious poetic consideration to an alternative, classical view:

> The undistinguish'd seeds of good and ill
>   Heav'n, in his bosom, from our knowledge hides;
> And draws them in contempt of human skill,
>   Which oft, for friends, mistaken foes provides.
>
> (ll. 141–4)

We have no skill to read such a fate. This point is repeated eloquently in a later stanza:

> In fortunes Empire blindly thus we go,
>   And wander after pathless destiny;

> Whose dark resorts since prudence cannot know
> In vain it would provide for what shall be.

(ll. 797–800)

However hard man may try to establish his own empires by trade or war, he remains a powerless wanderer in the inscrutable empire of Fortune, where his plans and achievements may be overturned at any moment, and where knowledge and foresight are impossible.

In *Annus Mirabilis*, then, there is an attempt to perceive and to understand, alongside a clear acknowledgement of the limitations of human perception, both physical and philosophical perception. The poem is interested in what is happening beyond the reach of our vision: there may be sand flats just below the surface of apparently deep water (ll. 450–2); fate is 'unseen' (l. 839); the fire was 'obscurely bred' (l. 858) but eventually became manifest:

> In this deep quiet, from what source unknown,
> Those seeds of fire their fatal birth disclose:
> And first, few scatt'ring sparks about were blown,
> Big with the flames that to our ruine rose.

(ll. 865–8)

The images of seeds and pregnancy are attempts to trap the inorganic world within the patterns of growth which we can understand from the organic world in which we, the observers, live. The same pressure behind the construction of explanations is evident in the accounts of the origins of precious stones and diamonds which Dryden has culled from the pages of the *Philosophical Transactions of the Royal Society*. 'Precious Stones at first are Dew, condens'd and harden'd by the warmth of the Sun, or subterranean Fires', he tells us in a note to line 10, and later he offers an explanation of the origins of gold:

> As those who unripe veins in Mines explore,
> On the rich bed again the warm turf lay,
> Till time digests the yet imperfect Ore,
> And know it will be Gold another day:

(ll. 553–6)

The organic metaphors ('digests', 'unripe') are attempts to interpret inorganic matter within the paradigms of the living world.

Dryden in his encomium to the Royal Society (ll. 657–64) sees its
work as an endeavour to

> behold the Law,
> And rule of beings in your Makers mind,
> And thence, like Limbecks, rich Idea's draw,
> To fit the levell'd use of humane kind.

> (ll. 661–4)

Art and science read nature in order to discern the divine laws by
which it operates, and thus further the useful arts of life (ll. 617–8).
Dryden's view of the Royal Society is in line with that of Thomas
Sprat in his *History*, who remarks that men are swayed too easily
by omens and prodigies; they need to dispel their superstitious
attitude to the natural world through acquiring proper knowledge:

> especially this last year, this gloomy, and ill-boding humor has
> prevail'd. So that it is now the fittest season for *Experiments* to
> arise, to teach us a Wisdome, which springs from the depths of
> *Knowledge*, to shake off the shadows, and to scatter the mists,
> which fill the minds of men with a vain consternation.[13]

Yet Dryden remains more sceptical, aware of the limitations of
language which is the only medium of human knowledge.

Annus Mirabilis deploys many of the prevailing myths of the
early Restoration: christianity, classical culture, the expansion of
trade, naval power and the intellectual imperialism of the Royal
Society. All these attempts to control and define life are evoked
with admiration, but they are juxtaposed with indications of the
problems of knowledge and poignant images of the human cost of
ambition. As no one myth dominates we are invited to construct
our own explanations from among those offered, and in so doing
we ponder the very activity of understanding. In this respect
Annus Mirabilis is a sceptical poem, revealing myths for what they
are – questionable human constructs. Roland Barthes wrote that
myth transforms what is particular and historical into the natural
and universal: 'myth is constituted by the loss of the historical
quality of things: in it, things lose the memory that they once were

made.'[14] The opposite happens in *Annus Mirabilis*: the poem attends closely to the historical particularity of events, foregrounding the processes of cultural fabrication and suggesting that in addition to the grand interlocking empires of military power, trade and science there may be a subversive counter-empire of Fortune in which imperialists can only wander blindly. The attempt to read history and power has involved Dryden in reflecting on the means of analysis and representation which he has at his disposal: his poetry probes the limitations of language and experiments with different classical models, resulting in a play of competing aesthetics and philosophies. Dryden's initial ventures into the role of author have entailed a self-conscious deployment of literary authorities and a loyal but astute depiction of political authority. An individual voice is already recognisable, one which insists on combining commitment and scepticism.

3
The Dramatist
1663–85

The writing of poetry could not secure a living for Dryden. It is unlikely that he earned anything much from his poems of the early 1660s, and it is probable that these pieces served chiefly to establish his name before the reading public and the men of power. If he was to make a reasonable income solely as a writer, Dryden would have to turn to the theatre, for no man of letters before Pope was able to make a living from poetry alone. Dryden's involvement with the theatre was often to prove burdensome and disillusioning, but there were several reasons why the theatre might have seemed attractive in these early years. The status of the playwright was no longer as disreputable as it had been when Shakespeare and Jonson had begun their careers: under Elizabeth playwrights had often been working actors, and actors were regarded at best as servants, at worst as vagabonds. The achievement of Jonson in gaining recognition for his plays as works of literature through their publication in a handsome folio collection in 1616 had helped to secure a similar recognition for Shakespeare in 1623 and for Beaumont and Fletcher in 1647. Without the canonisation of pre-war playwrights many play-texts would have been lost, and the literary reputations of their authors would have been harder to establish. For Dryden and his contemporaries this body of work was an impressive and even intimidating literary achievement. But the plays of the half-century before the civil war could not simply be revived for the new public, which had had few or no opportunities of theatre-going for twenty years. For reasons of taste as well as reasons of copyright a new repertoire had to be created, and those who were involved in this enterprise were men of substance and distinction. The two companies licensed by the King to perform plays were headed by Sir William Davenant, who had succeeded Jonson as poet laureate and already had an established record as a dramatist and producer, and Thomas Killigrew, diplomat and groom of the bedchamber to Charles II. New plays were provided by Abraham Cowley, at that time England's most celebrated poet, by the diplomat and Fellow of the Royal Society Sir Samuel Tuke, by the Earl of Orrery, an Irish grandee, and by Dryden's ambitious brother-in-law Sir Robert Howard. These new playwrights were gentlemen and aristocrats, and the creation of a new dramatic repertoire was an opportunity to fashion Restoration culture, building on and rivalling the early Stuart achievement, and thus helping to write out the Interregnum from public memory.

From the start Killigrew and Davenant were fierce competitors, and this competition shaped the course of Restoration drama. Killigrew had experienced actors and a large repertoire of pre-war plays; Davenant's troupe were novices and his repertoire meagre. With a monopoly shared by two companies, and a fairly limited London audience to draw upon, novelty would be vital. The quest for novelty led to the commissioning of new plays and to the development of more lavishly equipped theatres. Davenant's first theatre, the Duke's Playhouse, opened in 1661 in an adapted tennis court in Lincoln's Inn Fields which accommodated changeable scenery and machines: spectacle, song and dance were to be crucial in attracting audiences. Killigrew was forced to follow suit, and in 1663 he moved from his own converted tennis court in Vere Street to a new Theatre Royal between Bridges Street and Drury Lane. Although Cosimo III of Tuscany commented on a visit that 'the scenery is light, capable of a great many changes, and embellished with beautiful landscapes', it was evidently not lavish enough, and while the theatres were closed by the plague in 1666 Killigrew took the opportunity to widen the stage; Pepys picked his way through the debris to inspect 'the inside of the Stage and all the tiring roomes and Machines; and endeed it was a sight worth seeing.'[1] The Duke's Company, now managed by Thomas Betterton, moved in 1671 to a new theatre at Dorset Garden which had arrangements for even more elaborate scenic effects. Their mastery of spectacle was never matched by the King's Company, particularly after a fire destroyed the Theatre Royal in 1672; the replacement building, designed by Wren, was only 'a Plain Built House.'[2]

The development of Restoration drama was determined to a large degree by this rivalry between the two companies. As Robert Hume says:

Experienced writers almost invariably wrote specifically for one company or the other; consequently, they knew precisely what actors would be available and for what sort of roles. When one house did well, the other might try to steal its thunder (in Dennis's phrase) by imitation, or produce a novelty as a counter-attraction, or mock the success.

(p. 22)

There is, therefore, a strong element of self-consciousness in Restoration theatre. The redesigning of the playhouses away from the Elizabethan model, where an audience sat round three sides of the stage, to the proscenium arch design emphasised a formally framed spectacle, but this did not result in a loss of intimacy. Indeed, the audience was highly conscious of itself as a social group, and engaged in banter, intrigue and occasional brawls. The theatre's physical lines of demarcation mapped out social distinctions: the pit (the modern stalls) was dominated by the trend-setters who wished to display their wit and their fashions; the boxes (running above the pit, behind and alongside it) were occupied by the King, the courtiers and gentry; the middle gallery was the preserve of the middle classes; and the upper gallery was used by servants. The social composition of audiences was often played upon in prologues and epilogues which established a teasing relationship between playwright, actors and audience; sometimes the teasing descended to ritualised abuse, but it was always part of a well-recognised technique of audience management.[3]

Many of the prologues and epilogues to Restoration plays challenge the audience on the subject of judgment, exposing the vulnerability of the dramatist and actors to the audience's inattention or disapproval. In his early prologues Dryden dwells upon the difficulty of writing anything, since his predecessors have exhausted the available subjects:

> Our Poet yet protection hopes from you,
> But bribes you not with any thing that's new.
> Nature is old, which Poets imitate,
> And for Wit, those that boast their own estate,
> Forget *Fletcher* and *Ben* before them went,
> Their Elder Brothers, and that vastly spent:
> So much 'twill hardly be repair'd again.

('Prologue to *The Wild Gallant*', ll. 41–7)

The audience's criticism that the play lacks novelty is forestalled by the observation that nature itself (the subject of any writer) is old, and therefore does not admit of novelties; moreover, any wit has been used up by the earlier generation. This is more than a pre-emptive strike against hostile critics, for it expresses a real predicament for these new dramatists inheriting, as they put it, an estate which is virtually bankrupt. The desire for novelty led to an interest in the exotic, as the 'Epilogue to *The Indian Queen*' explains:

> You see what Shifts we are inforc'd to try
> To help out Wit with some Variety;
> Shows may be found that never yet were seen,
> 'Tis hard to finde such Wit as ne're has been:
> You have seen all that this old World cou'd do,
> We therefore try the fortune of the new,
> And hope it is below your aim to hit
> At untaught Nature with your practic'd Wit:
> Our naked Indians then, when Wits appear,
> Wou'd as soon chuse to have the Spaniards here:
> 'Tis true, y'have marks enough, the Plot, the Show,
> The Poets Scenes, nay, more the Painters too:
> If all this fail, considering the cost,
> 'Tis a true Voyage to the Indies lost:
> But if you smile on all, then these designs,
> Like the imperfect Treasure of our Mindes,
> 'Twill pass for currant wheresoe're they go,
> When to your bounteous hands their stamps they owe.

(ll. 1–18)

While this epilogue is a teasing reminder to the audience that the company has a large financial investment in these spectacular dramas set in Latin America, it is also an admission that spectacle may have to compensate for lack of 'wit' – a word which means here both 'intelligence' and 'liveliness of thought'. The naivety of the drama is like the naivety of the Indians it depicts; and the company is at the mercy of the sophisticated and financially powerful audience, just as the Indians are vulnerable to the conquering Spaniards. It is an image which, for all its playfulness, admits the subservience of art to the judgment of those who have the money. The epilogue is delivered from a position of superiority: few in the audience could match its witty couplets, none of the audience commands the actor's elevated position on the stage. Yet the command is temporary and precarious, for the audience may heckle, may doze off, may not return. Here the only independence seems to lie in continual play with the admissions of dependency. Dryden's 'Epilogue to *The Indian Emperour*' catalogues the various kinds of wit which different sections of the audience are allowed to judge – a classification which is at once flattering and sarcastic. As Dryden says in the 'Prologue to *Secret-Love*',

> Each Puny Censor, . . . his skill to boast,
> Is cheaply witty on the Poets cost.

(ll. 26–7)

yet at the same time

>   . . . you think your selves ill us'd
> When in smart Prologues you are not abus'd.

(ll. 35–6)

But none of this play can alter the poet's fundamental dependence upon the audience. In his 'Prologue to *An Evening's Love*' Dryden reflects upon the changing relationship which he has had with the theatre:

> When first our Poet set himself to write,
> Like a young Bridegroom on his Wedding-night
> He layd about him, and did so bestir him,
> His Muse could never lye in quiet for him:
> But now his Honey-moon is gone and past,
> Yet the ungrateful drudgery must last:
> And he is bound, as civil Husbands do,
> To strain himself, in complaisance to you:
> To write in pain, and counterfeit a bliss,
> Like the faint smackings of an after kiss.

(ll. 1–10)

The dramatist is bound by contract, and powerless to abridge his audience's freedom:

> Though now he claims in you an Husbands right,
> He will not hinder you of fresh delight.
> He, like a Seaman, seldom will appear;
> And means to trouble home but thrice a year:
> That only time from your Gallants he'll borrow;
> Be kind to day, and Cuckold him to morrow.
>
>   (ll. 30–5)

This is not quite Dryden's own voice: it is the company's dramatist speaking through an actor, extending the repertoire of the bantering relationship between servant and master. Yet it is also the voice of the playwright struggling for artistic integrity and financial survival.

Dryden's contract with the King's Company stipulated that he should deliver three plays a year. As a shareholder he would receive a portion of the company's profits, rather than having the playwright's third night's profits on each of his plays; and if he supplied prologues and epilogues for his colleagues' plays he could earn a few extra guineas. Dryden was a professional, bound by the practical limitations of his playhouse and company, and by the need to satisfy his audiences. If he was to satisfy himself artistically and intellectually it could only be through the use of – and creative play with – the conventions of the drama, which were in part dictated by audiences. Nevertheless, we should not imagine that Dryden was a frustrated romantic, longing for the opportunity for self-expression which the theatre denied him: convention enables speech, as well as limiting it, and for twenty years Dryden was influential in shaping both the forms and the ethos of Restoration drama, using it to make far-reaching enquiries into the ideologies and practices of his society. His work was generally successful commercially, and it is only in the mid 1670s that there is evidence that he had tired of the stage. He produced his plays at a steady rate, though not three a year: there were twenty-two plays between 1663 and 1683.[4] With *The Wild Gallant* (1663) he made an uncertain start: in its first version it was apparently insufficiently rakish, and Pepys commented that he did not know which of the characters was supposed to be the wild gallant.[5] Yet the assistance of the King's mistress, Lady Castlemaine, seems to have brought it to the attention of Charles himself, who had it acted at court. Little is known of the fate of *The Rival Ladies* (1664). *The Indian Queen* (1664) and its sequel *The Indian Emperour* (1665) successfully ex-

ploited exotic costumes and sets, and helped to set a fashion for the
rhymed heroic play. The comedies *Secret Love* and *Sir Martin
Mar-all* (both 1667) were unusually successful – Pepys saw the
latter ten times. In the same year the demand for music and
spectacle prompted a reworking of *The Tempest*. Dryden himself
thought *An Evening's Love* (1668) merely a fifth-rate play,[6] yet it ran
for a remarkable nine consecutive days. A further three heroic
plays were also well received: *Tyrannick Love* (1669) and the
two-part *The Conquest of Granada* (1670–1). Evidence is lacking about
the reception of what is now Dryden's best-known comedy,
Marriage A-la-mode (1671), though the subsequent comedy *The
Assignation; or, Love in a Nunnery* (1672) did not find favour, despite
its titillating setting. After the crude topical anti-Dutch play
Amboyna (1672?) Dryden, tiring of the stage, wrote his final heroic
play *Aureng-Zebe* (1675). Evidently he was casting around for new
directions at this period. He tried an operatic adaptation of *Paradise
Lost* (as *The State of Innocence*) which was never staged, and in 1677
produced *All for Love*, a version of the Antony and Cleopatra story
written with an eye on Shakespeare. His comedy *Mr Limberham*
(1678) was banned, though whether for political or moral reasons is
still unclear. Then *Oedipus* (1679) and *Troilus and Cressida* (1679)
continued Dryden's emulatory engagement with his great dramatic predecessors. His last three plays before a decade away from the
stage were politically topical: *The Spanish Fryar* (1680) includes
anti-papist satire, *The Duke of Guise* (1682) is a commentary on
Monmouth and the Whig cause, while the masque-like *Albion and
Albanius* (1685) celebrates the triumph of Charles II over his
enemies.

The audience for which Dryden was writing these plays was not
a self-conscious participant only during the recital of prologues
and epilogues. The style of performance encouraged an awareness
of different levels of theatrical representation. Audiences were,
first of all, aware of themselves, observing who sat with whom and
taking part in their own drama of critical and sexual by-play.
During a performance of *The Maid's Tragedy* Pepys found himself

> vexed all the while with two talking ladies and Sir Ch. Sidly, yet
> pleased to hear their discourse, he being a stranger; and one of
> the ladies would, and did, sit with her mask on all the play; and
> being exceedingly witty as ever I heard woman, did talk most
> pleasantly with him; but was, I believe, a virtuous woman and of

quality. He would fain know who she was, but she would not tell. Yet did give him many pleasant hints of her knowledge of him, by that means setting his brains at work to find out who she was; and did give him leave to use all means to find out who she was but pulling off her mask. He was mighty witty; and she also making sport with him very inoffensively, that a more pleasant rencontre I never heard. But by that means lost the pleasure of the play wholly, to which now and then Sir Ch. Sidlys exceptions against both words and pronouncing was very pretty.

(viii 71–2)

Pepys himself particularly admired Lady Castlemaine, and relished opportunities to observe her at the theatre. Sometimes there were little dramas involving her too; he was told by Mr Pierce of one occasion when

the King, coming the other day to his Theatre to see *The Indian Queene* (which he commends for a very fine thing), my Lady Castlemaine was in the next box before he came; and leaning over other ladies a while to whisper with the King, she ris out of that box and went into the King's and sat herself on the King's right hand between the King and the Duke of Yorke – which he swears put the King himself, as well as everybody else, out of countenance, and believes that she did it only to show the world that she is not out of favour yet – as was believed.

(v 33)

Pepys also admired, though not uncritically, the person and acting of Nell Gwyn, and was particularly interested in her performances in male costume, as in Dryden's *Secret Love*:

The King and Duke of York was at the play; but so great performance of a comical part was never, I believe, in the world before as Nell doth this, both as a mad girle and then, most and best of all, when she comes in like a young gallant; and hath the motions and carriage of a spark the most that ever I saw any man have. It makes me, I confess, admire her.

(viii 91)

Here Pepys is conscious of the audience, which includes Charles and James, and of both the skill and beauty of Nell Gwyn. On

several occasions Pepys had an opportunity to go backstage; he
was taken

> up into the Tireing-rooms and to the women's Shift, where Nell
> was dressing herself and was all unready; and is very pretty,
> prettier then I thought; and so walked all up and down the
> House above, and then below into the Scene-room . . . But Lord,
> to see how they were both painted would make a man mad – and
> did make me loath them – and what base company of men
> comes among them, and how lewdly they talk – and how poor
> the men are in clothes, and yet what a show they make on the
> stage by candle-light, is very observable.

> (viii 463)

The spectacle behind the scenes which is so very observable to
Pepys' curious gaze fascinates him partly because of the teasing
relationship which it has to the sights with which he is familiar on
stage. The private lives of the actors and actresses could hardly be
separated from their public performances when both men and
women were displayed as objects of sexual interest, the women's
allure often being enhanced and complicated by cross-dressing.
The audience's awareness of the players' sexuality could produce
intriguing use of both appropriate and unexpected casting. Nell
Gwyn, at a time when she was the King's mistress, played the
Emperor's daughter Valeria in *Tyrannick Love*, a play which was
supposedly a compliment to Charles' Queen Catherine. At the end
of the play as she is carried off stage dead, she rises and stops the
bearers:

> Hold, are you mad? you damn'd confounded Dog,
> I am to rise, and speak the Epilogue.

> (ll. 1–2)

And the epilogue plays teasingly with the mismatch between the
reputations of actress and character:

> . . . I dye
> Out of my Calling in a Tragedy.
> O Poet, damn'd dull Poet, who could prove
> So sensless! to make *Nelly* dye for Love . . .

> But, farewel Gentlemen, make haste to me,
> I'm sure e're long to have your company.

(ll. 15–26)

The invitation backstage is blatant. Blatant too was the way in which the play had earlier invited the audience to contemplate not merely the display but also the possible dismemberment of the woman's body, when the wheel on which St Catharine is to be martyred is revealed and Maximin orders:

> Go, bind her hand and foot beneath that Wheel:
> Four of you turn the dreadful Engine round;
> Four others hold her fast'ned to the ground:
> That by degrees her tender breasts may feel,
> First the rough razings of the pointed steel:
> Her Paps then let the bearded Tenters stake,
> And on each hook a gory Gobbet take;
> Till th' upper flesh by piece-meal torn away,
> Her beating heart shall to the Sun display.

(V i 245–53)

The audience's delight in the spectacle of stage machinery is tempered by their complicity in Maximin's sadistic erotic pleasure. The woman's body is available for sexual use, both on and off stage.

The game which Nell Gwyn played with the audience in that epilogue, and the teasing game which runs through *Tyrannick Love* when she is cast as a princess, are part of a self-conscious and stylised form of acting which characterises Restoration drama generally.[7] Such a playing style should not be confused with the affected voices and camp gestures which pass for authentic period style in some modern productions of Restoration comedy. It is true that comedy often quoted and parodied the foppish displays which were performed in the pit, but stylisation more importantly shapes the form of dramatic exchanges and the relationship between actor, words and audience. Restoration drama tended to prefer the exemplary: plots often have a diagrammatic shape which concentrates certain dilemmas for the characters, who are examples of particular forms of vice and virtue or the site where conflicting desires and duties struggle for mastery. Such plays tend therefore to neglect individual quirks and the particularities of experience; naturalistic presentation of character is not required. What is required instead is the rhetorical demonstration of states of mind. Words are not private utterances, but the typical language of a particular passion or dilemma, and they are voiced more for the benefit of the audience than for the other characters on stage; indeed, characters may often move downstage to speak lines out into the theatre away from their supposed interlocutors. Even when the drama is one of witty repartee or serious philosophical debate, the lines have a formality which marks them out as contributions to a dialectic which the audience is assessing, rather than to a naturalistically plausible confrontation with another person. Such a drama encourages the analysis of serious issues in generalised terms, and the dramas of individual lives are exemplifications of the forces which shape each human life: notably sexual passion, the power of the state, and the gods, fate or fortune.

*

Dryden's analysis of sexuality generally keeps away from any overt engagement with the particular sexual politics and *mores* of his own society; his analysis of contemporary sexuality proceeds at a deeper level because it declines to engage with the immediate social vocabulary. He avoids the apparent topicality of time, place and fashion which Etherege and Wycherley manipulate so discomfortingly. Instead of mapping the play of social conventions through which sexual desire is exhibited, controlled and satisfied, Dryden dramatises the force of the body's passions, the way in which women and men are bound by their physical selves, even while mind and spirit may aspire to lofty ideals or may attempt to impose moral and social duties which are at odds with the raw urgency of desire.[8] It is not only in his heroic plays that Dryden shows an awareness of the power of physical desire, for many of his translations from Ovid, Lucretius and Homer will explore that also. In his stage characters we already see how tragically human beings are bound to their bodies, and how fruitlessly they attempt to transcend their limitations. It is not simply that 'desire is boundless, and the act a slave to limit',[9] but that the body is subject to the demands of political expediency, the call of honour and duty, and the taboos which society places upon the accomplishment of some desires. The question of social taboo fascinated Dryden. Why does a particular society forbid sexual intercourse in certain cases? It is the complaint of Myrrha in the *Metamorphoses*, desiring her father Cinyras; and incest is the trap which awaits the unwitting lovers in *Don Sebastian* (1689).[10] But of special interest to Dryden is the uneasy relationship between the mind and the body. This is a philosophical concern which he may have encountered in Descartes, but certainly found in his avid reading of Montaigne. In the essay 'Upon some Verses of Virgil' Montaigne addresses the question of the representation of sexuality: intercourse 'is an action we have put in the precincts of silence, whence to draw it were an offence ... Nor dare we beare it but in circumlocution and picture'.[11] Why is this? Does not the concealment of sexuality in circumlocution, like the hiding of the genitals by clothing, arouse interest and desire rather than suppress them? Montaigne shows that the evasive means through which sexuality is represented are themselves problematic, perhaps even defeating the social ends which they claim to serve. In another essay, 'Of the force of imagination', Montaigne explores the ways in which the mind influences the body, causing impotence when it fears impotence, and performing successfully when reassured by some talisman. It was Montaigne who opened up for Dryden a world of different social customs, societies whose habits and taboos are so different from our own that they suggest that what we think of as being an eternal law of nature is only temporary human custom. Dryden was well aware that the drama of mind and body is a source of both comedy and tragedy for individuals, and a continual challenge to the writer who uses language to analyse and represent passion. But he also knew that in any society – and particularly in the Restoration – sexuality is always already politicised: there is no private space which is immune from governmental and social interference, no language of love and desire which is not already appropriated by society for its own ends of exploitation and control. That Dryden chose to set most of his plays abroad does not distance them from the sexually charged politics and politicised sexuality of his day: rather, it is this dislocation which enables his analysis.

In many of Dryden's heroic plays the drama arises precisely from the inevitable location of sexual desire within a political realm. *Secret Love* shows that sexual passion in a ruler (in this case the Queen of Sicily) is potentially a source of cruelty and tyranny.

Philocles and Candiope are in love, but the Queen is also in love
with Philocles. In Act III scene i the Queen contemptuously
describes to Philocles and other courtiers the deficiencies in
Candiope's beauty, and when the Queen leaves, Candiope responds to this tyranny by reflecting that

> The greatest slaves, in Monarchies, are they,
> Whom Birth sets nearest to Imperial sway.
> While jealous pow'r does sullenly o're spy,
> We play like Deer within the Lions eye.
> Would I for you some Shepherdess had been;
> And, but each May, ne're heard the name of Queen.

> (III i 166–71)

Philocles then proposes that they escape from court into a pastoral
paradise away from the Queen's surveillance:

> Since happiness may out of Courts be found
> Why stay we here on this enchanted ground?
> And choose not rather with content to dwell
> (If Love and we can find it) in a Cell?

> (III i 182–5)

But, unknown to Philocles, the Queen is herself eavesdropping on
the couple: even this talk of retirement is being policed. In any
case, Candiope realises the hold which political ambition has over
those who have once experienced power:

> Those who, like you, have once in Courts been great,
> May think they wish, but wish not to retreat.
> They seldom go but when they cannot stay;
> As loosing Gamesters throw the Dice away:
> Ev'n in that Cell, where you repose would find,
> Visions of Court will haunt your restless mind;
> And glorious dreams stand ready to restore
> The pleasing shapes of all you had before.

> (III i 186–93)

Though Philocles makes the expected rejoinder that 'All my

Ambition will in you be crown'd', the audience which is watching this debate about ambition and retirement is likely to agree with Candiope that 'Thus hope misleads it self in pleasant way.' And they would be right. The pull of ambition in Philocles is strong. He has enough honesty to admit that 'Int'rest makes all seem reason that leads to it' (IV i 317), and contemplates abandoning Candiope to marry the Queen. In soliloquy he observes:

> Where'er I cast about my wond'ring eyes,
> Greatness lies ready in some shape to tempt me.
> The royal furniture in every room,
> The Guards, and the huge waving crowds of people,
> All waiting for a sight of that fair Queen
> Who makes a present of her love to me:

> (V i 164–9)

and he asks an imaginary Stoic philosopher a rhetorical question:

> Now tell me, Stoique! — —
> If all these with a wish might be made thine,
> Would'st thou not truck thy ragged vertue for 'em?
> If Glory was a bait that Angels swallow'd
> How then should souls ally'd to sence, resist it?

> (V i 170–4)

The audience knows, of course, that a true Stoic philosopher *would* resist such temptation, and that it was only the fallen angels who swallowed the bait. The play of passion, the dilemma of souls 'ally'd to sence', is performed as an exemplary drama for the spectators to analyse.

At the end of the play the Queen announces that she will reward Philocles for his military service on her behalf; he imagines that she means to offer him herself in marriage, but instead she offers him Candiope, and he is struck silent. In an aside which exhibits his state of mind to the audience he admits how attractive the Queen appears to him; she has the attraction of power:

> I'm going to possess *Candiope*,
> And I am ravish'd with the joy on't! ha!
> Not ravish'd neither.

> For what can be more charming then that Queen?
> Behold how night sits lovely on her eye-brows,
> While day breaks from her eyes! then, a Crown too:
> Lost, lost, for ever lost, and now 'tis gone
> 'Tis beautiful! — —

                                                    (V i 426–33)

The Queen announces that she will remain unmarried and devote herself to the care of the people:

> As for my self I have resolv'd
> Still to continue as I am, unmarried:
> The cares, observances, and all the duties
> Which I should pay an Husband, I will place
> Upon my people; and our mutual love
> Shall make a blessing more than Conjugal.

                                                    (V i 456–61)

It is only when Philocles hears the Queen's resolution not to marry that he masters his jealousy and ambition, feelings which are political but expressed in sexual terms:

> Then, I am once more happy:
> For since none can possess her, I am pleas'd
> With my own choice, and will desire no more.
> For multiplying wishes is a curse
> That keeps the mind still painfully awake.

                                                    (V i 468–72)

Here tragedy is averted by renunciations, by the deliberate limitation of desire. Yet the accommodations which this ending arranges are not simply to be accepted by the audience without demur. The Queen's final action may be exemplary, but she has earlier been a disturbing example of the manipulative power which rulers may exercise, and an ending which suggests that the safest course is for a ruler's sexuality to be completely denied is hardly comforting to subjects of Charles II. In Philocles we see the mind torn between love and ambition, rewriting ambition as love, and expressing contentment in love only when ambition has been finally thwarted. As if to underline the arbitrariness of the truces which are made between reason and passion, the play does not end with this edifying spectacle, but moves on to a spirited negotiation between the lovers Florimell and Celadon (played by Nell Gwyn and Charles Hart) over the terms of their marriage contract:

> *Cel. Item*, I will have the liberty to sleep all night, without your interrupting my repose for any evil design whatsoever.
> *Flor. Item*, Then you shall bid me good night before you sleep.
> *Cel.* Provided always, that whatever liberties we take with other people, we continue very honest to one another.
> *Flor.* As far as will consist with a pleasant life.
> *Cel.* Lastly, Whereas the names of Husband and Wife hold forth nothing but clashing and cloying, and dulness and faintness in their signification; they shall be abolish'd for ever betwixt us.
> *Flor.* And instead of those, we will be married by the more agreeable names of Mistress and Gallant.

(V i 540–52)

This exchange was given a special character by the fact – known of course to Dryden and to many in the audience – that Gwyn and Hart had been lovers, and perhaps, early in 1667, still were. Nell Gwyn was in the process of being handed over to Lord Buckhurst, and in 1668 would be passed on to Charles II. *Secret Love* may draw back from explicit contemporary comment, but its depiction of the transactions between sexual desire and political ambition is not confined within the safe framework of the proscenium arch.

*

In *Aureng-Zebe* the lustful monarch is male, and here Dryden focuses on the image of the king as father of his people, which is one of the period's dominant ideological tropes. Aureng-Zebe loves Indamora, but so too does his father the Emperor. The Emperor confuses his roles: his instincts as a sexually predatory male lead him to want Indamora, and he is determined to have her – by force if necessary. Here the kingly power is entirely at the service of the private man's lust. The result is not only a misuse of power, but a neglect of the interests of his people and his son: fatherly care for country and child are subordinated to sexual passion. The Emperor's wife is also a victim of the despotic power which he insists husbands have over wives. Dryden repeatedly stresses this distortion of the traditional language, holding up the idea of patriarchy for sceptical scrutiny. Through showing the links which metaphor makes between these various areas of control, *Aureng-Zebe* makes visible the structures of power in a way which defeats the operation of ideology, which would use metaphor to have us accept the naturalness of these structures. We see the image as an image, a construction which performs a special service on behalf of those who have power. In *Aureng-Zebe* the Emperor's sexual licence is coercive of private bodies and destructive of the body politic. In an exchange between the Emperor and his son Morat, different ideas are voiced about power and pleasure. Morat likes fighting, and he also likes the display of kingly power:

> Methinks all pleasure is in greatness found.
> Kings, like Heav'n's eye, should spread their beams around,
> Pleased to be seen while glory's race they run;
> Rest is not for the chariot of the sun.

> (III i 166–9)[12]

The Emperor, however, is a degenerate form of Epicurean, preferring pleasure without the pains of government (either of the state or himself):

> Had we but lasting youth and time to spare,
> Some might be thrown away on fame and war.
> But youth, the perishing good, runs on too fast,
> And, unenjoyed, will spend itself to waste;
> Few know the use of life before 'tis past.
> Had I once more thy vigor to command,
> I would not let it die upon my hand.
> No hour of pleasure should pass empty by;
> Youth should watch joys, and shoot 'em as they fly.

> (III i 157–65)

This is more than an ironic representation of Charles II, for it keeps close to Lucretius, and is a dramatised version (albeit in a bastardised form) of a particular philosophy, one element in a theatrical and ethical dialectic for the audience to assess. Yet it is also a reflection on Charles, and when Morat remarks that

> Luxurious kings are to their people lost;
> They live like drones upon the public cost.

(III i 176–7)

or again,

> Women emasculate a monarch's reign,
> And murmuring crowds, who see 'em shine with gold,
> That pomp as their own ravished spoils behold.

(IV i 200–2)

many in the audience must have murmured agreement. But this is not an allegory; the Emperor is not Charles II; Morat is no virtuous critic of excess. Morat's words have a sharp, epigrammatic force, but they are also compromised by the character of their speaker. We are watching a play between different ways of living, one which through its philosophical generality and geographical distance can analyse the forces which shape the Restoration ethos, and through suggestive, discontinuous allusion can establish repeated contacts with the world just outside the theatre while maintaining an air of innocence.[13]

*

This form of drama can often create for itself a space in which the political theories of Restoration England can be debated philosophically, and given particular practical exemplification. In *The Conquest of Granada* the king, Boabdelin, whose authority is dubious since he has sworn an oath of allegiance to Ferdinand and Isabella of Spain, against whom he is in revolt, seeks to punish Almanzor for his intervention in a factional riot. Almanzor replies with a claim which provokes a debate on the nature of government:

> *Almanz.* No man has more contempt than I of breath
> But whence hast thou the right to give me death?
> Obey'd as Sovoraign by thy Subjects be,

But know, that I alone am King of me.
I am as free as Nature first made man
'Ere the base Laws of Servitude began
When wild in woods the noble Savage ran.
Boab. Since, then, no pow'r above your own you know,
Mankind shou'd use you like a common foe,
You shou'd be hunted like a Beast of Prey;
By your own law, I take your life away.
Almanz. My laws are made but only for my sake,
No King against himself a Law can make.
If thou pretend'st to be a Prince like me,
Blame not an act which should thy pattern be.
I saw th' opprest, and thought it did belong
To a King's office to redress the wrong:
I brought that Succour which thou oughtst to bring,
And so, in Nature, am thy Subjects King.
Boab. I do not want your Councel to direct,
Or aid to help me punish or protect.
Alm. Thou wantst 'em both, or better thou wouldst know
Then to let Factions in thy Kingdom grow.
Divided int'rests while thou thinkst to sway,
Draw like two brooks thy middle stream away:
For though they band, and jar, yet both combine
To make their greatness by the fall of thine.

(Part I, I i 203–29)

The debate here is a play between extreme positions. Almanzor
claims that man was born free, anticipating Rousseau. Civil society's laws are base servitude, and the savage is noble.[14] Here
Dryden is recalling the image of the noble and innocent natives
which Montaigne offers (without fully endorsing) in his essay 'Of
the Cannibals'. Boabdelin's rejoinder posits a different, Hobbesian,
notion of the state of nature, which is a war of every man against
every man, with no overall power to keep the peace. Since
Almanzor claims to be outside civil society, he can be hunted to
death as an outlaw. Almanzor retorts that the law is made for the
benefit of the individual, not to his detriment, and he then uses
Hobbes against Boabdelin: since he rather than Boabdelin has
provided these people with protection, he is their true sovereign.
Neither character holds a theoretical position which Dryden or his

audience would necessarily accept, but the argument succeeds in laying out the foundations of a debate about the legitimation of political authority in terms other than those of the divine right of kings, which was still the primary legitimising strategy in Restoration England. The remote setting, together with Boabdelin's uncertain status, enables Dryden to try out these arguments.

The reflections on government which these plays offer extend to a consideration of the imperialist adventure. Dryden's early plays *The Indian Queen* and *The Indian Emperour* use their setting in the Americas to mount a debate on nature and civilisation, taking their bearings partly from Montaigne. Queen Zempoalla provides several epigrammatic opinions on the way in which ideas of legitimacy may simply be a cover for the naked exercise of self-interest. The right of hereditary monarchs has its origin in violent usurpation:

> Let dull successive Monarchs mildly sway:
> Their conquering Fathers did the Laws forsake,
> And broke the old e're they the new cou'd make.

> (*The Indian Queen* III i 113–15)

But the observation is part of Zempoalla's attempt to excuse her own cruelty. Later, when her general observes that 'Princes are sacred', she replies:

> True, whilst they are free.
> But power once lost, farewell their sanctity.

> (III i 157–8)

Once princes diminish their power by taking advice from their subjects, they 'but like publick pageants move', reduced to player kings without power and so without sanctity. Divine right is but a rhetorical legitimation of power. Zempoalla's outburst here is due to an infatuation which prevents her taking advice, so once again the ideas are qualified by their speaker's interest. Nevertheless, the ideas are spoken.

The Indian Emperour takes this questioning further, and dramatises the clash between two cultures, that of the Mexican Indians under Montezuma, and that of the invading Spaniards led by Cortez. The hypocrisy of the Spaniards is evident in the formula by which Vasquez demands Montezuma's submission:

> *Spain*'s mighty Monarch, to whom Heaven thinks fit
> That all the Nations of the Earth submit,
> In gracious clemency, does condescend
> On these conditions to become your Friend,
> First, that of him you shall your Scepter hold,
> Next, you present him with your useless Gold:
> Last, that you leave those Idols you adore,
> And one true Deity with prayers implore.

> (I ii 266–73)

The interweaving of political, religious and economic imperialism could hardly be more blatant. Montezuma's reply exposes the duplicity of Vasquez's claim:

> You speak your Prince a mighty Emperour,
> But his demands have spoke him Proud, and Poor;
> He proudly at my free-born Scepter flies,
> Yet poorly begs a mettal I despise.
> Gold thou may'st take, what-ever thou canst find,
> Save what for sacred uses is design'd:
> But, by what right pretends your King to be
> This Soveraign Lord of all the World, and me?

> (I ii 274–81)

The Spaniards reply that the Pope has given Mexico to their king, and Montezuma comments:

> Ill does he represent the powers above,
> Who nourishes debate not Preaches love;
> Besides what greater folly can be shown?
> He gives another what is not his own.
> *Vasq.* His pow'r must needs unquestion'd be below,
> For he in Heaven an Empire can bestow.
> *Mont.* Empires in Heaven he with more ease may give,
> And you perhaps would with less thanks receive;
> But Heaven has need of no such Vice-roy here,
> It self bestows the Crowns that Monarchs wear.

> *Piz.* You wrong his power as you mistake our end,
> Who came thus far Religion to extend.
> *Mont.* He who Religion truely understands
> Knows its extent must be in Men, not Lands.

(I ii 285–98)

The Spaniards never manage to muster convincing replies, and Montezuma's incisive, epigrammatic speeches carry the day (at least in terms of argument: the Spaniards eventually win by murder). This debate about religious imperialism is skewed against the Spaniards partly to provide comfortable anti-catholic material for a protestant audience, but the argument also reflects generally upon the European imperialistic adventure, showing the ways in which self-interest is legitimised. At the beginning of the play Vasquez had commented on the poverty of the country:

> Corn, Wine, and Oyl are wanting to this ground,
> In which our Countries fruitfully abound:
> As if this Infant world, yet un-array'd,
> Naked and bare, in Natures Lap were laid.
> No useful Arts have yet found footing here;
> But all untaught and salvage does appear.

(I i 5–10)

Cortez corrects him:

> Wild and untaught are Terms which we alone
> Invent, for fashions differing from our own:
> For all their Customs are by Nature wrought,
> But we, by Art, unteach what Nature taught.

(I i 11–14)

And Pizarro contradicts Vasquez's assertion that Spain is fruitful:

> In *Spain* our Springs, like Old Mens Children, be
> Decay'd and wither'd from their Infancy:
> No kindly showers fall on our barren earth,
> To hatch the seasons in a timely birth.

(I i 15–18)

There is a recognition here that European ways are not normative, and as the play develops we see clearly the hypocrisy of imperialist rhetoric. Cortez claims:

> Heaven from all ages wisely did provide
> This wealth, and for the bravest Nation hide,
> Who with four hundred foot and forty horse,
> Dare boldly go a New found World to force.
>
> (I i 31–4)

The emphasis appropriately falls on 'force'.

At the beginning of *The Conquest of Granada*, Part II, King Ferdinand has a curious speech on the growth and decay of empire:

> When Empire in its Childhood first appears,
> A watchful Fate o'resees its tender years;
> Till, grown more strong, it thrusts, and stretches out,
> And Elbows all the Kingdoms round about:
> The place thus made for its first breathing free,
> It moves again for ease and Luxury:
> Till, swelling by degrees, it has possest
> The greater space; and now crowds up the rest.
> When from behind, there starts some petty State;
> And pushes on its now unwieldy fate:
> Then, down the precipice of time it goes,
> And sinks in Minutes, which in Ages rose.
>
> (I i 5–16)

Ferdinand intends to say that heaven and earth are joining to free Spain from Islam, but the terms which he uses imply that the growth and decay of empire is like that of a human being, who will in due course be rudely jostled aside by some more thrusting competitor. Oblivion is its ultimate fate. Dryden's plays often end with gestures which reassure: the legitimate ruler is triumphant at the end of *The Conquest of Granada*, the true heir is recognised and restored in *Marriage A-la-mode*. But during the course of the plays, through the licence given by the dialectic of drama, Dryden has asked some far-reaching questions about the operations of power, and the strategies which it uses to give itself authority.

4
The Critic
1668–84

The sense of a new beginning which is manifest in the public poems and the new dramatic repertoire of the early 1660s is evident too in the development of the critical essay, a form which Dryden rapidly mastered and made the medium for a debate over the theory and practice of drama. The self-consciousness which Dryden displayed as a dramatist, able to manipulate a complex and shifting relationship between stage and audience, is applied here to defining the identity of the age for which he is working, seeking to understand and explain how the new culture differs from the old, and what the tasks are which confront a writer at this particular time. The essays are often polemical, justifying various technical practices such as the use of rhyme in heroic drama, but they also campaign for a sense of the special character and achievement of Restoration culture. The critical preface was not invented by Dryden: Jonson had written prefaces and prologues which justified his art against ignorant misreading, and during the republic writers such as Cowley, Davenant, Denham and Hobbes had set out their ideas about the heroic poem or the theory of translation. But in Dryden's hands the preface becomes a way of defining and shaping contemporary culture, and in so doing establishing Dryden's own position as the period's dominant man of letters.

Dryden's first critical treatise, *An Essay of Dramatick Poesie* (1668), is a discussion of English drama, and, more broadly, of the ways in which the critical and literary practices of other cultures (ancient Greece and Rome, contemporary France and Spain, and particularly pre-war England) might provide models for writers in the Restoration. The essay is cast in the form of a debate between friends who take a boat down the Thames, but their literary conversation takes place against the backdrop of war:

It was that memorable day, in the first Summer of the late War,

67

when our Navy ingag'd the *Dutch*: a day wherein the two most
mighty and best appointed Fleets which any age had ever seen,
disputed the command of the greater half of the Globe, the
commerce of Nations, and the riches of the Universe ... the
noise of the Cannon from both Navies reach'd our ears about the
City: so that all men, being alarm'd with it, and in a dreadful
suspence of the event, which they knew was then deciding,
every one went following the sound as his fancy led him ... all
seeking the noise in the depth of silence.

(xvii 8)

The evocation of war is not casual: by beginning his essay with this
danger to national survival Dryden suggests the fragility of the
contemporary world, and the following essay is haunted by the
memory of past conflicts. The shadow of the civil war falls across
English history and separates the men of the 1660s from their
literary predecessors. If the political fate of the nation is hanging in
the balance at this moment, so too is its cultural future. The seven
years since the Restoration had seen vigorous activity in the arts
and sciences, and the successful re-establishment of the theatre,
but there was as yet hardly any work which could stand comparison with the achievements of the other cultures which Dryden and
his contemporaries took as models. England had to prove herself
in the playhouse as well as in the theatre of war.

The *Essay* is not written in Dryden's own person, but presents a
play of different voices, giving appropriate expression to the
teasing, testing scepticism of Dryden's mind. The four friends are
called Eugenius, Crites, Lisideius and Neander, names which
half-conceal the identities of several prominent writers. Eugenius
('well born') may be Charles Sackville, later Earl of Dorset, to
whom the *Essay* is dedicated; Crites ('critical') is primarily a portrait
of Sir Robert Howard; the name Lisideius is a Latinised anagram of
Sir Charles Sedley (or Sidley); and Neander ('the new man')
represents Dryden himself. Thus Dryden advertises – though with
all due modesty – his connections with the leading contemporary
men of letters, while not having to attribute specific opinions to
individuals. Dryden may ensure that Neander has some strong
arguments, but he nevertheless allows a play of different opinions,
and self-deprecatingly ends the essay with Neander so caught up
in what he is saying that he fails to notice that the boat has arrived
back at Somerset stairs.

Neander, the new man, knows that his period is a new time which requires a fresh examination of the principles and practices that have been inherited from previous writers. In *Astraea Redux* and *To His Sacred Majesty* Dryden had written that a new kind of time had been inaugurated by the return of Charles II, but when he came to write *Annus Mirabilis* he was conscious of the difficulty of understanding man's place in time, exploring the competing interpretations of life as governed by providence or crossed by fortune, and aware of the dangerous contingency of life lived in history. *An Essay of Dramatick Poesie* is similarly troubled by time. It begins with an ironic glance at the involvement of poets with current events, deriding those opportunists who have a poem ready for every eventuality:

> There are some of those impertinent people of whom you speak, answer'd *Lisideius*, who to my knowledg, are already so pro-vided, either way, that they can produce not onely a Panegirick upon the Victory, but, if need be a funeral elegy on the Duke:
>
> (xvii 9)

Crites deplores the degeneracy of contemporary poetry, lamenting that 'there are so few who write well in this Age ... they neither rise to the dignity of the last Age, nor to any of the Ancients' (xvii 12). But Eugenius disagrees:

> If your quarrel ... to those who now write, be grounded onely on your reverence to Antiquity, there is no man more ready to adore those great *Greeks* and *Romans* than I am: but on the other side, I cannot think so contemptibly of the Age in which I live, or so dishonourably of my own Countrey, as not to judge we equal the Ancients in most kinds of Poesie, and in some surpass them; neither know I any reason why I may not be as zealous for the Reputation of our Age, as we find the Ancients themselves were in reference to those who lived before them.
>
> (xvii 12–13)

A debate threatens over the relative merits of ancients and mod-erns, a favourite topic in Europe at this time, but when Crites suggests that they limit themselves to the drama, Eugenius points out that the discussion will have to take account not only of the classics but also of plays by the pre-war dramatists, for 'those we now see acted, come short of many which were written in the last Age' (xvii 13).

The terminology of 'the present age' and 'the last age' which pervades this essay points to the Restoration as a new period set apart from the miseries of civil war, but also remote now from the supposedly golden age of Elizabethan and early Stuart culture. This is partly a recoil from the millennial vocabulary of the 1650s, an insistence that there are other, less apocalyptic ways of conceiving of one's own time and of understanding the place of that period in history. Dryden is not simply stating that the Restoration period (for which he had no other name than 'this age') is different from the past, but debating whether the change has brought progress. Crites argues that:

> It has been observed of Arts and Sciences, that in one and the same Century they have arriv'd to great perfection; and no wonder, since every Age has a kind of Universal Genius, which inclines those that live in it to some particular Studies: the Work then being push'd on by many hands, must of necessity go forward.
>
> Is it not evident, in these last hundred years (when the Study of Philosophy has been the business of all the *Virtuosi* in *Christendome*) that almost a new Nature has been reveal'd to us? that more errours of the School have been detected, more useful Experiments in Philosophy have been made, more Noble Secrets in Opticks, Medicine, Anatomy, Astronomy, discover'd, than in all those credulous and doting Ages from *Aristotle* to us? so true it is that nothing spreads more fast than Science, when rightly and generally cultivated.
>
> (xvii 15)

But Crites does not perceive a comparable development in poetry, because nowadays it is not sufficiently esteemed to make writers wish to excel at it. In this case, the ancients were in direct contact with a nature which the moderns know only at secondhand:

> Those Ancients have been faithful Imitators and wise Observers of that Nature which is so torn and ill represented in our Plays, they have handed down to us a perfect resemblance of her; which we, like ill Copyers, neglecting to look on, have rendred monstrous and disfigur'd.
>
> (xvii 16)

Eugenius has been listening to Crites with growing impatience, and retorts that the moderns' attitude to the ancients lacks

> neither veneration nor gratitude while we acknowledge that to overcome them we must make use of the advantages we have receiv'd from them; but to these assistances we have joyned our own industry ... We draw not therefore after their lines, but those of Nature; and having the life before us, besides the experience of all they knew, it is no wonder if we hit some airs and features which they have miss'd ... for if Natural Causes be more known now then in the time of *Aristotle*, because more studied, it follows that Poesie and other Arts may with the same pains arrive still neerer to perfection.
>
> (xvii 22)

Although the friends disagree in their analysis of Restoration literature, they do share two important assumptions which are key recurring premises in Dryden's critical thinking. The first is that rapid cultural changes have been taking place which affect the way contemporaries value the opinions and achievements of their predecessors. Like the men of the Renaissance, newly aware of their difference from those who lived in the 'middle ages', men in the Restoration are aware that a decisive shift has taken place which alters their perception of their place within history. The second is that underneath these changes (whether they are construed as progress or decay) 'Nature' is constant and unchanging, universally accessible in every age to scientific inquiry and to poetic representation.

Though Eugenius is given the better of the argument, this dialectic between the progess and the decay of poetry does not quite come to a resolution, for Crites and Eugenius eventually declare a truce and the discussion moves on to another instance of the problem of locating the present within a cultural tradition. Neander raises the relationship of contemporary poets to their Jacobean and Caroline predecessors:

> They are honour'd, and almost ador'd by us, as they deserve; neither do I know any so presumptuous of themselves as to contend with them. Yet give me leave to say thus much, without injury to their Ashes, that not onely we shall never equal them, but they could never equal themselves, were they to rise and write again. We acknowledge them our Fathers in wit, but they

have ruin'd their Estates themselves before they came to their childrens hands.

(xvii 72–3)

This image of Restoration dramatists as children who find that they have nothing to inherit is a particularly desolate version of the familiar metaphor of a poetic lineage of fathers and sons, an image which even to a pre-Freudian age sufficiently figured the trauma inherent in the struggle to establish a separate identity, a distinctive voice for oneself within a language which is always already shaped by the masters of the previous generation.[1]

Yet there is a play here between loss and gain. Because cultural conditions have changed, even the father-figures of pre-war drama would be unable to match their own achievements now. As Neander says, 'the Genius of every Age is different', and the particular achievement of the later seventeenth-century has been to refine the language of social intercourse and to perfect the metre of English verse (xvii 73). But even with this assurance of a superiority in some areas, Dryden's essay is troubled by the brooding presences of his great dramatic precursors, Beaumont, Fletcher, Jonson and Shakespeare. Shakespeare dominates:

> he was the man who of all Modern, and perhaps Ancient Poets, had the largest and most comprehensive soul. All the Images of Nature were still present to him, and he drew them not laboriously, but luckily: when he describes any thing, you more than see it, you feel it too. Those who accuse him to have wanted learning, give him the greater commendation: he was naturally learn'd; he needed not the spectacles of Books to read Nature; he look'd inwards, and found her there. I cannot say he is every where alike; were he so, I should do him injury to compare him with the greatest of Mankind. He is many times flat, insipid; his Comick wit degenerating into clenches, his serious swelling into Bombast. But he is always great, when some great occasion is presented to him.

(xvii 55)

Like the ancient writers who were close to Nature, Shakespeare had 'all the Images of Nature ... present to him', enjoying an unmediated contact with the world in all its manifestations. Represented here in the terms with which critics were characterising Homer,[2] Shakespeare is credited with an 'original genius', a natural intelligence and insight which did not need to use many books. Jonson, by contrast, is the laboriously learned student of classical literature:

> He was deeply conversant in the Ancients, both *Greek* and *Latine*, and he borrow'd boldly from them... But he has done his Robberies so openly, that one may see he fears not to be taxed by any Law... perhaps too, he did a little too much Romanize our Tongue, leaving the words which he translated almost as much *Latine* as he found them: wherein though he learnedly followed their language, he did not enough comply with the Idiom of ours. If I would compare him with *Shakespeare*, I must acknowledge him the more correct Poet, but *Shakespeare* the greater wit. *Shakespeare* was the *Homer*, or Father of our Dramatick Poets; *Johnson* was the *Virgil*, the pattern of elaborate writing.
>
> (xvii 57–8)

That Dryden can think of comparing Shakespeare and Jonson with Homer and Virgil indicates his confidence in his native culture, but at the same time it underlines his predicament as a modern writer cowed by their achievement. To avoid being reduced to speechlessness, Dryden places these giants historically as well as mythically, and in so doing creates an historically specific cultural position from which he can work. Within each of these descriptions there is a movement between the eternal and the contingent. Shakespeare is in touch with Nature herself, yet he shares his period's reprehensible addiction to grandiloquence and word-play; Jonson is solidly read in the classics, yet fails to translate his knowledge into idiomatic English. Their timeless understanding, which Dryden figures through images of 'depth' and 'presence', is marred by the historical contingency of having to write in an imperfect language. The harshnesses of that language have been smoothed away in the half-century since they were writing. Civility is one of the hallmarks of the new age, and Jonson inevitably appears crude when judged by the new standards of a refinement which is both social and linguistic:

> They, who have best succeeded on the Stage,
> Have still conform'd their Genius to their Age.
> Thus *Jonson* did Mechanique humour show,
> When men were dull, and conversation low.

> Then, Comedy was faultless, but 'twas course . . .
> If Love and Honour now are higher rais'd,
> 'Tis not the Poet, but the Age is prais'd.
> Wit's now arriv'd to a more high degree;
> Our native Language more refin'd and free.[3]

*

The prologues and prefaces in which Dryden explored his art established him as the leading critical voice of his day, and in spite of the modesty of his rhetoric Dryden soon found that others resented his dominance. The early 1670s saw an uncomfortable number of satires and critiques.[4] In *The Rehearsal* (1672) the Duke of Buckingham guyed Dryden on stage as the vain and absurd dramatist Mr Bayes; a group of books beginning with *Remarques on the Humours and Conversations of the Town* (1673) include Dryden amongst those whose works have contributed to the decline of morality, marriage and religion; and *The Censure of the Rota on Mr Driden's Conquest of Granada* (1673) began a critical debate on Dryden's poems and plays. Dryden did not trouble to reply directly to any of these squibs, but they taught him the cost of exposing himself to public criticism. He did, however, engage in a substantial debate with Thomas Shadwell which occupied many of their critical prefaces, prologues and epilogues for ten years.

There were several issues which occupied Dryden and Shadwell, including the status of the heroic drama, but most of the discussion centred on Jonson and his significance for contemporary writers. Central to Dryden's critical position is the recognition that times change, cultures develop, and the language through which society conducts its affairs is never constant. Every writer is at once confined by and enabled by the linguistic resources of his age. Jonson himself had adopted a respectful but not subservient attitude to the classics, saying:

> I know *Nothing* can conduce more to letters, then to examine the writings of the *Ancients*, and not to rest in their sole Authority, or take all upon trust from them . . . For to all the observations of the *Ancients*, wee have our owne experience: which, if wee will use, and apply, wee have better meanes to pronounce. It is true they open'd the gates, and made the way, that went before us; but as Guides, not Commanders.[5]

If we turn back further to Horace himself (in *Epistle* II i) we find him defending what was for him modern poetry against unthinking reverence for the ancients. So Dryden is in fact taking up an appropriately classical position in attempting to fashion a modern poetics through the critical assessment of past writers. It is Shadwell who, in his uncritical reverence for Jonson and his opportunistic appropriation of Jonsonian precedents for his own work, is being unclassical in spirit. Shadwell's criticism tends to assert eternal rules, quoting Horace as a universal authority and setting up Jonson's work as a paradigm of comic art for every age. Dryden, by contrast, seems aware that both ancient and modern classics exist in and for their own times; he is wary of dogmatism, and in place of rules prefers *ad hoc* definitions and the practical analysis of examples.[6] He also admits his own imperfections, while Shadwell seems unaware of the embarrassing gap between the claims of his prefaces and the achievements of the plays themselves.

Dryden's attitude to Jonson is critical but not hostile. In the Preface to *An Evening's Love* (1671) he writes:

> I know I have been accus'd as an enemy of his writings; but without any other reason than that I do not admire him blindly, and without looking into his imperfections. For why should he only be exempted from those frailties, from which *Homer* and *Virgil* are not free? Or why should there be any *ipse dixit* in our Poetry, any more than there is in our Philosophy? I admire and applaud him where I ought: those who do more do but value themselves in their admiration of him: and, by telling you they extoll *Ben. Johnson*'s way, would insinuate to you that they can practice it.
>
> (x 205)

This is a clear blow at Shadwell.

Dryden and Shadwell differed particularly over the proper form and function of comedy. Should Jonson provide an example for imitation? Jonsonian humours comedy had been a form of social and psychological analysis, a humanistic mode of representing the follies of mankind through concentrated, extravagant examples of those passions (the humours) which make human beings grotesque and obsessive. This is the form of comedy which Shadwell claimed to be using as a medium of moral education, saying that 'a

Poet ought to do all that he can, decently to please, that so he may instruct.'[7] He explains his purposes in the Preface to *The Royal Shepherdess* (1669):

> the Rules of Morality and good Manners are strictly observed in it: (Vertue being exalted, and Vice depressed) and perhaps it might have been better received had neither been done in it: for I find, it pleases most to see Vice incouraged by bringing the Characters of debauch'd people upon the Stage, and making them pass for fine Gentlemen who openly profess Swearing, Drinking, Whoring, breaking Windows, beating Constables, &c. and that is esteem'd among us a Gentile gayety of Humour, which is contrary to the Customs and Laws of all civilized Nations. But it is said, by some, that this pleases the people, and a Poets business is onely to endeavour that: But he that debases himself to think of nothing but pleasing the Rabble, loses the dignity of a Poet, and becomes as little as a Jugler, or a Rope-Dancer; who please more then he can do: but the office of a Poet is,
>   *Simul & jucunda, & idonea dicere vitae.*[8]

Shadwell particularly attacks the form of comedy which Dryden practised, the comedy of wit and repartee:

> I have known some of late so Insolent to say, that *Ben Johnson* wrote his best *Playes* without Wit; imagining, that all the Wit in *Playes* consisted in bringing two persons upon the Stage to break Jests, and to bob one another, which they call *Repartie*, not considering that there is more wit and invention requir'd in the finding out good Humor, and Matter proper for it, then in all their smart reparties . . . in the *Playes* which have been wrote of late, there is no such thing as perfect Character, but the two chief persons are most commonly a Swearing, Drinking, Whoring, Ruffian for a Lover, and an impudent ill-bred *tomrig* for a Mistress, and these are the fine people of the *Play*; and there is that Latitude in this, that almost any thing is proper for them to say; but their chief Subject is bawdy, and prophaness, which they call *brisk writing*, when the most dissolute of Men, that relish those things well enough in private, are *chok'd* at e'm in publick: and, methinks, if there were nothing but the ill Manners of it, it should make Poets avoid that Indecent way of Writing.[9]

The most extensive defence which Dryden made of his own
practice, the Preface to *An Evening's Love*, begins with the dis-
arming claim that any reputation which he may acquire through
writing comedy is of little consequence to him, and that the
successes which he has had in pleasing the audience through low
comedy give him little satisfaction. But he takes pains to distinguish between comedy and farce:

> Comedy consists, though of low persons, yet of natural actions,
> and characters; I mean such humours, adventures, and de-
> signes, as are to be found and met with in the world. Farce, on
> the other side, consists of forc'd humours, and unnatural events.
> Comedy presents us with the imperfections of humane nature:
> Farce entertains us with what is monstrous and chimerical.
>
> (x 203)

Shadwell's plays, he implies, are of the latter, farcical kind, and in
Mac Flecknoe Shadwell will be said to have 'promis'd a Play and
dwindled to a Farce' (l. 182). Dryden admits that in *An Evening's
Love* he has 'given too much to the people ... and am asham'd for
them as well as for my self, that I have pleas'd them at so cheap a
rate', saying that 'I love to deal clearly and plainly, and to speak of
my own faults with more criticism, than I would of another Poets'
(x 204). But he is not prepared to concede too much:

> Yet I think it no vanity to say that this Comedy has as much of
> entertainment in it as many other which have bin lately written:
> and, if I find my own errors in it, I am able at the same time to
> arraign all my Contemporaries for greater. As I pretend not that I
> can write humour, so none of them can reasonably pretend to
> have written it as they ought.
>
> (x 204)

And he will not admit that the main function of comedy is to be
morally elevating:

> 'Tis charg'd upon me that I make debauch'd persons ... happy
> in the conclusion of my Play; against the Law of Comedy, which
> is to reward virtue and punish vice. I answer first, that I know no
> such law to have been constantly observ'd in Comedy, either by
> the Ancient or Modern Poets.
>
> (x 208)

Dryden aptly cites Jonson's *Alchemist*, where the ending is far from rewarding the virtuous and punishing the villainous. Shadwell has simplified Jonson, and simplified classical critical theory into a crude version which seems to suit his own procedures. Dryden denies that classical critics expected comedy to be concerned to instruct:

> the business of the Poet is to make you laugh: when he writes humour he makes folly ridiculous; when wit, he moves you, if not always to laughter, yet to a pleasure that is more noble. And if he works a cure on folly, and the small imperfections in mankind, by exposing them to publick view, that cure is not perform'd by an immediate operation. For it works first on the ill nature of the Audience; they are mov'd to laugh by the representation of deformity; and the shame of that laughter, teaches us to amend what is ridiculous in our manners.
>
> (x 209)

In citing Horace and Jonson in support of his argument, Dryden is resisting Shadwell's claim to be the steward of the classical heritage for his own times. That is hardly a role which Dryden would have claimed for himself, at least at this early period, but there is nevertheless a detectible irritation in Dryden's writing at having to defend his practice against the ostensible authority of classical and neo-classical writers.

Dryden and Shadwell conducted their debate with a curious form of courtesy, forbearing to name each other, yet using paraphrases which are scarcely polite. Shadwell often uses a deceptive plural ('some of late so Insolent to say, that *Ben Johnson* wrote his best *Playes* without Wit') and when he refers specifically to Dryden he prefaces his disagreement with an elaborate and convoluted compliment which is deflated before it is finished:

> I must . . . take liberty to dissent from my particular friend, for whom I have a very great respect, and whose Writings I extreamly admire; and though I will not say his is the best way of writing, yet, I am sure, his manner of writing it is much the best that ever was.[10]

Dryden also uses plurals, together with passive constructions which tend to efface Shadwell from the discussion as much as possible ('there is another crime with which I am charged . . .'), and though he too can dispense compliments ('Some ingenious men, for whom I have a particular esteem', where the plural now disperses the compliment) the vocabulary of the Preface to *The Assignation* indicates how precarious this politeness is: 'old Opiniatre judges' . . . 'my enemies' . . . 'those who can judge of neither' . . . 'Mountebank' . . . 'an ill-natur'd judge' . . . 'enemies of Repartie' (x 202–7). The mask of politeness was to slip altogether in Shadwell's Preface to *The Virtuoso* (1676):

> Nor do I hear of any profest Enemies to the Play, but some Women and some Men of Feminine understandings, who like slight Plays onely, that represent a little tattle sort of Conversation like their own; but true Humour is not liked or understood by them, and therefore even my attempt towards it is condemned by them. But the same people, to my great comfort, damn all Mr. *Johnson*'s Plays, who was incomparably the best Drammatick Poet that ever was, or, I believe, ever will be.[11]

Dryden had had enough. He retaliated in the devastating satire *Mac Flecknoe*, which was composed in the summer of 1676 and put into limited circulation in manuscript.[12] This method of publication confined the poem to London literary circles, sparing Shadwell the more public humiliation of print, but ensuring a knowledgeable and influential readership. Whereas Shadwell had claimed in his prefaces to be the true heir of Ben Jonson, *Mac Flecknoe* reconstructs him as the son of Richard Flecknoe, the vacuously prolific versifier, dramatist and critic who himself had Jonsonian pretensions. Shadwell turns out to be Jonsonian only in his bulk and his fondness for the bottle. The poem begins with Flecknoe retiring from his position as ruler over the empire of dullness:

> All humane things are subject to decay,
> And, when Fate summons, Monarchs must obey:
> This *Fleckno* found, who, like *Augustus*, young
> Was call'd to Empire, and had govern'd long:
> In Prose and Verse, was own'd, without dispute
> Through all the Realms of *Non-sense*, absolute.

(ll. 1–6)

Shadwell is a fitting successor to Flecknoe, as helped along by ale
and opium he produces meaningless plays, experiencing 'Pangs
without birth, and fruitless Industry' (l. 148). His coronation procession through the seedier quarters of London winds its way past
the sorry contents of booksellers' stalls:

> No *Persian* Carpets spread th' Imperial way,
> But scatter'd Limbs of mangled Poets lay:
> From dusty shops neglected Authors come,
> Martyrs of Pies, and Reliques of the Bum.
> Much *Heywood*, *Shirley*, *Ogleby* there lay,
> But loads of *Sh* – – – – – – almost choakt the way.

> (ll. 98–103)

So the great project of establishing an Augustan culture in Restoration England has been blighted by the activities of writers such as
Flecknoe and Shadwell who turn everything which they touch into
dross; their products are mere excrement. In this realm works of
literature are good only for lining pie-dishes or wiping arses.
Though sharply pointed, *Mac Flecknoe* is not just a personal
lampoon but a reappropriation of the classical heritage from one
who had turned its principles into mechanical rules, and had
refused to see that only a more imaginative recreation of classical
aims could help contemporary writers. Dryden thought that Jonson had only imperfectly translated his classical sources into a
native English idiom, but Shadwell resorts to large-scale pillaging:

> When did his Muse from *Fletcher* scenes purloin,
> As thou whole *Eth'ridg* dost transfuse to thine?
> But so transfus'd as Oyl on Waters flow.

> (ll. 183–5)

Jonson's language may have been harsh, but in Shadwell's hands
the language has degenerated into empty word-play:

> Leave writing Plays, and chuse for thy command
> Some peacefull Province in Acrostick Land.
> There thou maist wings display and Altars raise,
> And torture one poor word Ten thousand ways.

> (ll. 205–8)

Shadwell enjoys an orderly succession from father to son, an apparently effortless continuity within the eternal kingdom of dullness: 'Of his Dominion may no end be known', says Flecknoe of his heir (l. 141). This is itself a parodic version of Shadwell's inability to comprehend the nature of cultural change. His role is to 'wage immortal War with Wit' (l. 12), to maintain an eternal war against development, contingency and the birth of fresh thinking.

*

During the early 1680s Dryden was occupied with several plans for making the English language and English poetry a fitting element of the new culture. Concerted projects were organised by Dryden and his publisher Jacob Tonson to translate the classics,[13] bringing these texts into a contemporary idiom for a new readership, while Dryden was also associated with the group of writers around the Earl of Roscommon who were planning to emulate the Académie Française and refine the English language. In 1684 Roscommon published his *Essay on Translated Verse*, to which Dryden contributed a commendatory poem. Like the critical prefaces of the previous two decades, this poem is fascinated by the origin and development of the arts:

> Whether the fruitful *Nile,* or *Tyrian* Shore,
> The seeds of Arts and Infant Science bore,
> 'Tis sure the noble Plant, translated first,
> Advanc'd its head in *Grecian* Gardens nurst.
> The *Grecians* added Verse, their tuneful Tongue
> Made Nature first, and Nature's God their song.
> Nor stopt Translation here: For conquering *Rome*
> With *Grecian* Spoils brought *Grecian* Numbers home;
> Enrich'd by those *Athenian* Muses more,
> Than all the vanquish'd World cou'd yield before.

(ll. 1–10)

But there is now a stronger confidence in the English achievement than there had been in 1668. As Greek culture was translated to Rome, so classical culture is being translated to Restoration England:

> The Wit of *Greece,* the Gravity of *Rome*
> Appear exalted in the *Brittish* Loome;

> The Muses Empire is restor'd agen,
> In *Charles* his Reign, and by *Roscommon's* Pen.

> (ll. 26–9)

The advice which Roscommon gives about translation is offered modestly, not dogmatically, in the spirit of Horace rather than of Shadwell:

> Yet modestly he does his Work survey,
> And calls a finish'd Poem an *ESSAY*;
> For all the needful Rules are scatter'd here;
> Truth smoothly told, and pleasantly severe.

> (ll. 30–3)

New English writers may meet their predecessors as equals and incorporate them into their new culture; they will

> On equal terms with ancient Wit ingage,
> Nor mighty *Homer* fear, nor sacred *Virgil's* page:
> Our *English* Palace opens wide in state;
> And without stooping they may pass the Gate.

> (ll. 75–8)

Such confidence in 1684 must have been partly political, arising from the King's defeat of the opposition in the Exclusion Crisis of 1680–2, but it can also be attributed to the new interest in making translations from the classics which was currently leading several writers to put Latin and Greek poetry into the English tongue. But Dryden still had mixed feelings about the capacities of English; it was being refined, but it was still unstable. In the Preface to *Troilus and Cressida* in 1679 Dryden had compared Shakespeare with Aeschylus, and observed:

> In the Age of that Poet, the *Greek* tongue was arriv'd to its full perfection; they had then amongst them an exact Standard of Writing, and of Speaking: the *English* Language is not capable of such a certainty; and we are at present so far from it, that we are

wanting in the very Foundation of it, a perfect Grammar. Yet it must be allow'd to the present Age, that the tongue in general is so much refin'd since *Shakespear*'s time, that many of his words, and more of his Phrases, are scarce intelligible.

(xiii 225)

This lack of a grammar which would give precision and stability to the English language in a time of historical flux led Dryden to compose a promotional poem in 1684 for Lewis Maidwell's Latin grammar, which, he thought, would help to make Latin a stable guide to English:

> Latine is now of equal use become
> To Englishmen, as was the Greek to Rome:
> It guides our language, nothing is exprest
> Gracefull or true but by the Roman test.

(ll. 1–4)

In Maidwell's method the teaching of language also gives his students a grasp of history:

> That at the last Historians they become
> And know the deeds as well as words of Rome.

(ll. 33–4)[14]

The cultural project urged in the *Essay of Dramatick Poesie,* whereby the language and literature of England become a modern counterpart to those of ancient Greece and Rome, is now something which Dryden sees actually taking shape.

But this achievement, as Dryden continually points out, is fashioned within historical processes, and as such is vulnerable to the contingencies which both empower and frustrate writers. Fortune may strike at any moment to destroy a talent. In December 1683 the gifted young poet John Oldham died of smallpox, and Dryden composed a memorial poem for him which speaks eloquently of the tragedy of a writer's life cut short:

> Farewel, too little and too lately known,
> Whom I began to think and call my own;
> For sure our Souls were near ally'd; and thine

Cast in the same Poetick mould with mine.
One common Note on either Lyre did strike,
And Knaves and Fools we both abhorr'd alike:
To the same Goal did both our Studies drive,
The last set out the soonest did arrive.
Thus *Nisus* fell upon the slippery place,
While his young Friend perform'd and won the Race.
O early ripe! to thy abundant store
What could advancing age have added more?
It might (what Nature never gives the young)
Have taught the numbers of thy native Tongue.
But Satyr needs not those, and Wit will shine
Through the harsh cadence of a rugged line.
A noble Error, and but seldom made,
When Poets are by too much force betray'd.
Thy generous fruits, though gather'd ere their prime
Still shew'd a quickness; and maturing time
But mellows what we write to the dull sweets of Rime.
Once more, hail and farewel; farewel thou young,
But ah too short, *Marcellus* of our Tongue;
Thy Brows with Ivy, and with Laurels bound;
But Fate and gloomy Night encompass thee around.

Dryden's poem is classical in its poise and its imagery, casting Oldham as Marcellus, the designated heir of Augustus who was struck down when still young. It is classical too in its stoical refusal of Christian immortality, a remarkable translation of Roman feeling into English verse. Along with the judicious critical appraisal of Oldham's strengths and limitations there is a passionate regret, evident in the disturbed rhythms, which cannot acquiesce in this wanton destruction. Oldham is mourned in his own right, but he also stands for any writer, and for the current hopes of English poetry. Moreover, Dryden writes himself into the poem through the allusion to the Virgilian story of Nisus and Euryalus, in which the older man slipped during a race, leaving his young friend to succeed. Oldham has achieved in his own classical translations the kind of work which Dryden was aiming at but had not yet accomplished. Oldham was young, but his talent was already ripe; maturing time would only have mellowed his voice, and perhaps taken the fire out of his language. Time which enables cultural change is now its destroyer. Alongside Dryden's careful discus-

sions of the public writer taking his part in historical development
and co-operative effort, we now meet the disrupting image of the
empire's heir stricken by fate, alone, and hidden from our view by
impenetrable night.

*

For all the prominence which Dryden gives to the role of the writer
in these essays and poems, there is a modesty and self-effacement
in his rhetoric. It is seldom simply his own work which is being
promoted or defended, but a whole collaborative endeavour.
Dryden accords particular prominence here to the aristocracy, and
it is clear that the conditions of contemporary patronage made it
imperative for him to extol the literary skills and financial generos-
ity of meagrely talented grandees such as Roscommon and Dorset.
His plays carry dedications to a dozen dukes and earls, as well as
other members of the nobility and gentry. Facile compliment is the
price which a writer has to pay for sheer survival, let alone modest
advancement, in a society dominated by hereditary privilege, but
Dryden does seem to have believed that some of these lords had a
real part to play in Restoration culture. As he says to Roscommon:

> How will Invention and Translation thrive
> When Authors nobly born will bear their part
> And not disdain th' inglorious praise of Art!
>
> (ll. 54–6)

Others besides Roscommon were making their mark: the Earl of
Mulgrave translated one of Ovid's *Heroides* and penned an *Essay
upon Poetry* and an *Essay upon Satire* (for which Dryden was beaten
up);[15] the Earls of Dorset and Rochester were writing songs and
satires; noble patronage helped several theatrical careers.

Dryden's longing for a civilised aristocratic literary community is
seen most strikingly in the Dedication to *The Assignation*, where he
reminds Sir Charles Sedley of the cultured evenings which they
have spent together, occasions reminiscent of the convivial meetings celebrated by Horace:

Certainly the Poets of that Age enjoy'd much happiness in the
Conversation and Friendship of one another. They imitated the

best way of Living, which was to pursue an innocent and inoffensive Pleasure ... We have, like them, our Genial Nights; where our discourse is neither too serious, nor too light; but alwayes pleasant, and for the most part instructive: the raillery neither too sharp upon the present, nor too censorious on the absent; and the Cups onely such as will raise the Conversation of the Night, without disturbing the business of the Morrow.

(xi 320–1)

Besides the pride in keeping aristocratic company which this essay exhibits, there is also a rejoinder to Shadwell here, showing him that classicism is a matter of the spirit rather than the letter. (Shadwell was to have his revenge by brutally rewriting Dryden's account of his behaviour in polite company in *The Medal of John Bayes*, quoted in Chapter 5.) But Dryden could be scathing in his contempt for those frivolous and malicious lords whose writings contributed nothing to the lasting achievement of English letters but much to the bitchiness, rivalry and debauchery which tainted the Restoration court. In the Preface to *All for Love* Dryden makes clear his feelings about the Earl of Rochester and others of his ilk:

is not this a wretched affectation, not to be contented with what Fortune has done for them, and sit down quietly with their Estates, but they must call their Wits into question, and needlesly expose their nakedness to publick view? ... while they are so eager to destroy the fame of others, their ambition is manifest in their concernment: some Poem of their own is to be produc'd, and the Slaves are to be laid flat with their faces on the ground, that the Monarch may appear in the greater Majesty.

Dionysius and *Nero* had the same longings, but with all their power they cou'd never bring their business well about. 'Tis true, they proclaim'd themselves Poets by sound of Trumpet; and Poets they were upon pain of death to any man who durst call them otherwise.

Rochester and his associates exercise their privileged position tyrannically, not aiding genuine talent, but exacting sycophantic praise from real writers for their own feeble verses; they ape Nero rather than Maecenas, the celebrated patron of Horace:

we see how happily it has succeeded with him; for his own bad Poetry is forgotten, and their Panegyricks of him still remain. But they who should be our Patrons, are for no such expensive ways to fame: they have much of the Poetry of *Maecenas*, but little of his liberality. They are for persecuting *Horace* and *Virgil*, in the persons of their Successors, (for such is every man, who has any part of their Soul and Fire, though in a lesse degree.) Some of their little *Zanies* yet go farther; for they are Persecutors even of *Horace* himself, as far as they are able, by their ignorant and vile imitations of him; by making an unjust use of his Authority, and turning his Artillery against his Friends. But how would he disdain to be Copyed by such hands!

(xiii 14–16)

Dryden carefully refrains from naming Rochester, but his target is clear from several allusions and half-quotations throughout the preface,[16] in particular the reference to Rochester's *An Allusion to Horace*, the imitation of Horace's *Satire* I x in which Rochester criticised Dryden for the way his plays pandered to their audiences. In the end, the only defence which the writer has against the abuse of literature and literary patronage by vain and witty aristocrats is to trust that his work will outshine and outlast theirs.

In all these critical essays Dryden's voice continually modulates into various different modes according to the decorum demanded by the occasion, but he sounds a particularly personal note in the dedication to the Earl of Mulgrave which is prefixed to *Aureng-Zebe* (1676). In it Dryden expresses dissatisfaction with his career as a public writer. Praising Mulgrave for his disdain for the factional quarrels of court life, he continues:

Neither am I formed to praise a court, who admire and covet nothing but the easiness and quiet of retirement ... True greatness, if it be anywhere on earth, is in a private virtue, removed from the notion of pomp and vanity, confined to a contemplation of itself, and cent'ring on itself ... The truth is, the consideration of so vain a creature as man is not worth our pains. I have fool enough at home without looking for it abroad, and am a sufficient theater to myself of ridiculous actions, without expecting company either in a court, a town, or playhouse.

He has wearied of the stage, and intends to turn his attention to an epic poem:

> I desire to be no longer the Sisyphus of the stage, to roll up a stone with endless labor (which, to follow the proverb, gathers no moss) and which is perpetually falling down again. I never thought myself very fit for an employment where many of my predecessors have excelled me in all kinds, and some of my contemporaries, even in my own partial judgment, have outdone me in *comedy*. Some little hopes I have yet remaining (and those too, considering my abilities, may be vain) that I may make the world some part of amends for many ill plays by an heroic poem.[17]

The writing of an heroic poem was thwarted, however, not by any lack of abilities on Dryden's part, but his failure to find patronage. Reflecting dejectedly on this abandoned project in 1693 he recalled that:

> being encourag'd only with fair Words, by King *Charles* II, my little Sallary ill paid, and no prospect of a future Subsistance, I was then Discourag'd in the beginning of my Attempt.[18]

What might easily have been the crowning glory of Restoration culture never materialised. Charles was no Maecenas, no Augustus. Though Dryden always remained loyal to his ungrateful master, he was to devote much of his writing to the absurdities and tyrannies of those who wield power.

5
The Political Writer
1678–85

'Hired to Lye and Libel':[1] Shadwell's description of Dryden's role as a political writer may be extreme, but essentially the same judgment is found in several contemporary pamphlets and not a few modern accounts of Dryden's political writing. Readers often cling to the notion that great writers should be unsullied by any commitment to partisan politics, particularly to conservative positions. But 'politics' in the reign of Charles II had little in common with modern politics (except that of Northern Ireland), for it entailed a bitter and bloody debate over the very survival of the nation as a particular religious entity. When, in the preface to *Absalom and Achitophel* Dryden observed that 'he who draws his Pen for one Party, must expect to make Enemies of the other. For, *Wit* and *Fool*, are Consequents of *Whig* and *Tory*: And every man is a Knave or an Ass to the contrary side' (ll. 3–5), he was responding to the very recent transformation of politics into a factional dispute. In the first two decades of Charles' reign there had been a politics of acquiescence if not of consensus, with religious dissent marginalised and fragmented, and the economic self-interest of various individuals and groups in Parliament finding expression in shifting alliances. After the puritans had been driven into a form of internal exile under the church settlement of 1661–2, the question of what status and freedom could be permitted to them was raised from time to time, but generally in the context of the King's attempts to improve the legal position of catholics. Parliament usually remained firmly of the opinion that dissenters – whether puritans or catholics – were not to be entrusted with the conduct of state affairs or the education of the young. Much of the politics of the 1660s and 1670s revolved around the question of whether the King and his ministers were to be trusted to guard a protestant nation. There was unease about any attempt to fashion close ties with France, that bastion of catholicism and absolutism, but also fear of the commercial power of the Dutch. When Charles did decide on war with the Netherlands it was executed with considerable expense and less than conspicuous success. 'Politics' was a series of manoeuvres in Parliament designed to keep the King on the strait path of protestantism and of government by consent of the aristocracy and bourgeoisie.

Dryden's overtly political writing never departed from a firm adherence to Charles II in particular and the Stuart house in general. *Astraea Redux, To His Sacred Majesty,* and *Annus Mirabilis* all celebrate the person and good government of the King. But *Annus Mirabilis* not only extols Charles' care for his people, it makes him acknowledge his own failings, and the poem engages with the troubling questions which attend the exercise of imperial power. So too Dryden's plays of the subsequent decade address questions of legitimacy and tyranny. Dryden in the 1670s may have been Poet Laureate and Historiographer Royal (albeit with a small and irregularly paid salary) but he was no royal lapdog, and there were at least some contemporaries who thought of him as an oppositional writer.[2] If this was untrue, it nevertheless attests his independence.

The configuration of people's allegiances was transformed in the years from 1678 to 1683 by the Popish Plot and the Exclusion Crisis. The Popish Plot was a mixture of farce and melodrama which eventually claimed many lives, and profoundly affected attitudes towards religion and politics for a generation. In the summer of 1678 the renegade clergyman Titus Oates claimed that there was a plot, masterminded by the Jesuits, to assassinate the King, overturn the government, and impose catholicism by force of arms. The details of this plot emerged piecemeal, as various 'witnesses' surfaced or as Oates 'remembered' more details. Tragically there was enough genuine evidence of conspiratorial activity by the Duke of York's former secretary Edward Coleman to provide substance to Oates' allegations; fear and venality provided the rest. During the last months of 1678 and through much of 1679 inquiries, trials and executions heightened rather than allayed public insecurity, and it was in this atmosphere of half-justified paranoia that the issue of the succession to the throne was re-opened. Since Charles lacked any legitimate children, his heir was his younger brother James, Duke of York, who was a catholic. The previous catholic ruler of England, 'bloody' Mary, had presided over a slaughter of protestants whose martyrdom was enshrined in the national memory. Many were unwilling to trust that

James would be more tolerant than Mary, or could keep the Inquisition at bay. The idea that *cuius regio, eius religio* ('the country follows its ruler's religion') was too prevalent in contemporary Europe. What was at stake went beyond matters of religious doctrine and practice, vital though these were, for it was the nation's very identity which was threatened. According to the prevailing mythology, England was a protestant land where the people pursued their own religion free of interference from a foreign pope who would demand both secular and ecclesiastical control. Accordingly efforts were made to exclude James from the succession, or to set up some form of regency which would effectively remove power from his hands.

Spurred on by the alarming disclosures of Titus Oates, Parliament regarded this as an urgent priority. In 1679 a bill asserted that James had been seduced by the Pope's agents, was promoting the interests of France, and should be excluded from the succession. Charles dissolved that parliament, and delayed summoning its successor, but the year from October 1679 to October 1680 brought little reduction in the political temperature: rather, debate was conducted all the more violently in coffee houses and ale houses, on the streets, and through a vigorous pamphlet war. The opposition to James was a rough coalition of different interests, including disgruntled aristocrats, city traders and closet republicans, and there was no such thing as a 'Whig party'. Nevertheless, the Whigs were well organised, bringing together their supporters through a network of meeting-places and linking London with the provinces through the efficient dissemination of newsletters and pamphlets. Co-ordinating much of this activity was the Earl of Shaftesbury, assisted by the philosopher John Locke and others with a gift for pamphlet controversy and clandestine organisation. London was particularly good ground for the Whigs, for it valued its traditional independence from royal interference; loyal to Parliament during the civil war, it still had its merchants zealous for protestantism and profits, and its apprentices who were not averse to the occasional riot. The watchwords of the Whigs were 'liberty' and 'property'; they were defending the people's protestantism against the threat of catholic despotism, and their lives and goods against a predatory absolutist monarchy. Some (but not all) of the Whigs would have been sympathetic to the Miltonic position that kings are entrusted with power by a sovereign people, who may resume it if their trust is abused. On the other side the 'Tory' coalition is harder to define, but it included the anglican establishment, much of the judiciary, nobility and gentry: these adhered to the Stuart doctrine of the divine right of kings, and the inalienable hereditary succession to the crown. Their rhetoric drew on biblical precedents and claimed that the King's authority had been given to him by God; it could not be altered by merely human intervention.

When Parliament was finally permitted to meet in 1680, the Commons passed a bill which not only excluded James from the succession but declared him guilty of high treason if he should return to England. (Charles had consigned him to discreet exile in Brussels and Edinburgh.) The Lords rejected the bill after fierce debate, but the issue would not go away. Charles dissolved Parliament again and summoned a new one to meet in the spring of 1681 at Oxford, away from the unhealthily Whiggish influences of London. Disregarding Oxford's atmosphere of somnolent conservatism, the Commons turned once more to debate the succession, while in the Lords the Earl of Shaftesbury attempted to persuade Charles to make his illegitimate son Monmouth heir to the throne in James' stead. Charles refused. He could now afford to spurn all Parliament's anxious proposals since he had just concluded a secret agreement with France for huge annual subsidies. No longer did he need to rely upon Parliament to vote him taxes, which it was only inclined to do if it could obtain satisfactory guarantees about the succession. After just one week the Oxford Parliament was dissolved, and henceforward Charles would govern without a parliament for the rest of his reign.

But the political struggle was not over: it moved back to London, where Charles now felt strong enough to move on to the offensive. Shaftesbury was arrested in July and charged with high treason, but when the case came to a preliminary hearing in November the jury returned a verdict of *ignoramus* ('we do not know'), indicating that there was insufficient evidence to proceed to a full trial by the House of Lords. Like the charge, the verdict was politically motivated. Juries were selected by local sheriffs, and these reflected the Whig ethos in London. Charles therefore began a campaign against the independence of local government both in London and across the country, rescinding charters and reconstituting local authorities so as to give the crown firmer control. Trials began to convict Whig activists, and as the executions went on, Shaftesbury decided to retire to the safer climate of Holland.

The political struggle was conducted not only in Parliament but across London and the country by means of a huge pamphlet war. The quantity of publications dated 1680 is matched only by that of 1648 (the execution of Charles I in old-style dating) and 1660 (when there was a great debate about the demise of the republic and the return of the monarchy).[3] Public opinion was crucial, and readers were saturated with newspapers and propaganda sheets, sermons urging obedience, constitutional arguments from lawyers and historians, manifestos for parliamentary elections, petitions and addresses to the King, verbatim transcripts of trials, lurid accounts of plots, murders and executions, along with ballads and satires of varying degrees of indecency. Dryden's writing from this period took its place in this mêlée, and although we now read his poems in the sober form of scholarly editions, they were originally circulated as pamphlets, jostling for the attention of readers on booksellers' shelves alongside *The Country-mans Complaint*, *The Badger in the Fox-Trap* or *The Character of a Modern Whig*.

Dryden was slow to engage in the cut-and-thrust of partisan politics. He did so first through his prologues and epilogues, which were addressed to theatre audiences. In the Epilogue to *Troilus and Cressida*, performed in April 1679, Dryden allowed Thersites to joke about the Popish Plot while attempting to defend the theatrical plot which the audience had just seen; if the plot has been poor, at least he has not confessed to it:

> If guilty, yet I'm sure oth' Churches blessing,
> By suffering for the Plot, without confessing.

(ll. 27–8)

This irreverence is in character for Thersites, but it is Dryden who is seizing the opportunity to suggest that the Popish Plot is as much of a fiction as any dramatic plot. On other occasions Dryden was more explicit. His Prologue to Tate's *The Loyal General* (1680) equates sound political views with sound literary judgment:

> If yet there be a few that take delight
> In that which reasonable Men should write;
> To them Alone we Dedicate this Night.
> The Rest may satisfie their curious Itch
> With City Gazets or some Factious Speech,
> Or what-ere Libel for the Publick Good,
> Stirs up the Shrove-tide Crew to Fire and Blood!

(ll. 1–7)

Those who do not appreciate the labours of rational men had better confine themselves to reading about Whig city politics, or taking part in the ritual apprentices' riot on Shrove Tuesday. Such malcontents will stage their own drama:

> . . . you turn Players on the Worlds great Stage,
> And Act your selves the Farce of your own Age.

> (ll. 33–4)

Dryden implies that the Tory cause is aligned with culture and rationality, while the Whigs are irrational philistines whose preferred recreations are watching rope-dancing or burning the pope in effigy (ll. 10–11). In the Prologue which was spoken in July 1680 on the annual visit of the King's Company to Oxford, Dryden foresees a time when puritan enthusiasm may drive out learning altogether:

> And few years hence, if Anarchy goes on,
> *Jack Presbyter* shall here Erect his Throne.
> Knock out a Tub with Preaching once a day,
> And every Prayer be longer than a Play.
> Then all you Heathen Wits shall go to Pot,
> For disbelieving of a Popish Plot:

> (ll. 11–16)

When Charles and his Parliament came to Oxford in March 1681 the players came too, and Dryden wrote a special prologue for a performance in front of the King. The rhetoric is ostensibly the opposite of factional, for it urges peace and concord:

> This Place the seat of Peace, the quiet Cell
> Where Arts remov'd from noisy buisness dwell,
> Shou'd calm your Wills, unite the jarring parts,
> And with a kind Contagion seize your hearts:
> Oh! may its Genius, like soft Musick move,
> And tune you all to Concord and to Love.
> Our Ark that has in Tempests long been tost,
> Cou'd never land on so secure a Coast.

From hence you may look back on Civil Rage,
And view the ruines of the former Age.
Here a New World its glories may unfold,
And here be sav'd the remnants of the Old.

(ll. 11–22)

But the partisan aim is scarcely concealed. Opposition is represented as nothing but a noisy and wilful turbulence which can be soothed away by the arts; Oxford is valued not only for its culture but also for its history as a royalist refuge during the civil war, a war which the Whigs are in danger of repeating. At about the same time Dryden composed a Prologue and Epilogue for the occasion when the King and Queen attended a performance of John Banks' *The Unhappy Favourite*. The Prologue suggests that Englishmen are restlessly pursuing novelty for its own sake; political upheaval is caused by a spiritual disease:

Tell me you Powers, why should vain Man pursue,
With endless Toyl, each object that is new,
And for the seeming substance leave the true—
Why should he quit for hopes his certain good,
And loath the Manna of his dayly food?
Must *England* still the Scene of Changes be,
Tost and Tempestuous like our Ambient Sea?
Must still our Weather and our Wills agree?
Without our Blood our Liberties we have,
Who that is free would Fight to be a Slave?
Or what can Wars to after Times Assure,
Of which our Present Age is not secure?
All that our Monarch would for us Ordain,
Is but t' Injoy the Blessings of his Reign.
Our Land's an *Eden*, and the Main's our Fence,
While we Preserve our State of Innocence;
That lost, then Beasts their Brutal Force employ,
And first their Lord, and then themselves destroy:
What Civil Broils have cost we know too well,
Oh let it be enough that once we fell,
And every Heart conspire with every Tongue,
Still to have such a King, and this King Long.

(ll. 13–34)

The present offers certain good; liberties are secure and do not need to be fought for; England is a stable, paradisal state which is in danger of becoming the domain of beasts of prey. Contrasting present stability with the restless pursuit of change by the Whigs, Dryden draws a picture of a current state of freedom and innocence whose long continuance should be the earnest prayer of every subject.

*

Dryden's most decisive entry into the politics of party and faction came with *Absalom and Achitophel*, published on 17 November 1681 in order to influence public opinion in advance of Shaftesbury's trial. Dryden is so often remembered by this one poem that we need to recall just how atypical it is in his oeuvre. Under the pressure of an urgent political crisis, Dryden's sceptical, philosophical intelligence narrowed somewhat to counter an immediate threat to what he believed in. In the previous twenty years of his writing career Dryden had never eschewed controversy, but neither had he sought it. In literary debates he often conceded the force of opposing views and declined to descend to routine abuse. His political poems had been interested in the nation, its identity, its ethos and its survival. He was a late contributor to the paper war between the factions, and his prologues are mild in comparison with the robust work of his contemporaries. After the Exclusion Crisis had passed Dryden would not again engage in party controversy. Nor was his poetic vein primarily a satiric one: scepticism and irony were more his modes. Unlike its sequel *The Medall*, which carries the subtitle 'A Satyre against Sedition', *Absalom and Achitophel* is described simply as 'A Poem', which slyly leaves the reader to discover its genre and subject.

In applying the biblical story of Absalom's rebellion against King David to the Whig campaign for a protestant succession, Dryden was drawing upon a familiar association of Charles and David which had been deployed by poets and preachers since 1660.[4] But in Dryden's hands the story assumed a special significance. First, it suggested that the Whig campaign was a rebellion against the King rather than a crusade to preserve English liberties from a potentially predatory James II. Second, it acknowledged Charles' sexual exploits (which had given widespread offence) but also suggested that they were mild in comparison with those of David, who had arranged the murder of Uriah in order to obtain his wife. James, the central figure in this crisis, is astutely given no biblical equivalent, thus avoiding the embarrassment of having to represent him and define his role and intentions. Absalom, the King's beloved but undutiful son, aptly figures the Duke of Monmouth, and by breaking away from the biblical story before the death of Absalom the poem both warns of disaster and invites an alternative ending. Achitophel the crafty councillor provides Dryden with a memorable persona for Shaftesbury, while other more-or-less appropriate names from other parts of the Bible are assigned to other leading Whigs and Tories.

Just as Dryden was not the first to associate Charles with David, so he was not the first to compare Shaftesbury with Achitophel or Monmouth with Absalom, and much of the imagery in the portraits of the Whig leaders has close parallels in the pamphlets and poems which were currently circulating.[5] But novelty was not Dryden's aim: almost the reverse. He wished rather to have his readers recognise familiar individuals and images rearranged in a persuasive new configuration, and indeed the number of echoes, allusions and rejoinders which the poem provoked indicates how forcefully Dryden promoted his own interpretation of events.

It was one thing to call the opposition rude names, even rude names culled from the Bible; it was another to construct a narrative which translated the messy contingencies of current politics into a story which could be read as a single and coherent whole. The use of a biblical typology was Dryden's solution: by imposing upon current events a narrative which had an existing, familiar shape (known to all readers of the Bible, which meant to everyone) together with an already familiar, authorised interpretation (through which the story was recognised to speak of God's providential care for his kings), Dryden aimed to translate Monmouth, Shaftesbury and their associates out of the realm of constitutional debate and political manoeuvring into a fixed world where their actions were subjected to a single, final interpretation. The Whigs, who insisted upon their freedoms, their ability to control events, their right to change the divinely determined succession, and their need to insure against an uncertain future, were inserted by Dryden into a typology from which they had no escape, a story over which they had no control. It was this command of an ostensibly authoritative narrative which distinguished *Absalom and Achitophel* from its rivals. A typological narrative carries with it little or no liberty of interpretation, for the private voice of the reader cannot speak against the quasi-divine voice of the typology: while a typology may be recorded by a fallible scribe, it claims to be a pattern which God himself has written into history for man to discern. Readers of *Absalom and Achitophel* were intended to be limited to working out the contemporary application of each biblical name (about which there was general agreement in all but a few cases) and pondering the appropriateness of Dryden's choices. The author thus dictates the interpretation of his text, and the text controls the interpretation of events. By rewriting the events of the moment in terms of a biblical paradigm, *Absalom and Achitophel* implies that this moment in history is to be read as an example of an ancient and recurring narrative – the story of the wilful rebel who defies his God and King.

Absalom and Achitophel moves adroitly between different time schemes. The opening passage locates David's sexual adventures in a golden age before clerical tyranny:

> In pious times, e'r Priest-craft did begin,
> Before *Polygamy* was made a sin;
> When man, on many, multiply'd his kind,
> E'r one to one was, cursedly, confind:
> When Nature prompted, and no law deny'd
> Promiscuous use of Concubine and Bride;
> Then, *Israel*'s Monarch, after Heaven's own heart,
> His vigorous Warmth did, variously, impart
> To Wives and Slaves: And, wide as his Command,
> Scatter'd his Maker's Image through the Land.
>
>   (ll. 1–10)

The poem then passes into a different kind of time, a narrative of civil war which moves between English history and the supposedly Davidic period, with an evocation of a third time, even more remote and mythically powerful, which is that of Adam's rebellion against God in the Garden of Eden:

> These *Adam*-wits, too fortunately free,
> Began to dream they wanted libertie;
> And when no rule, no president was found
> Of men, by Laws less circumscrib'd and bound,

They led their wild desires to Woods and Caves,
And thought that all but Savages were Slaves.
They who when *Saul* was dead, without a blow,
Made foolish *Ishbosheth* the Crown forgo;
Who banisht *David* did from *Hebron* bring,
And, with a Generall Shout, proclaim'd him King:

(ll. 51–60)

(Saul and Ishbosheth stand for Oliver and Richard Cromwell.)

The poem then moves into a present tense in which the characters of Absalom and Achitophel are analysed; they converse together and plot David's downfall. This present tense is almost what the reader would recognise as his own political present, but there is a schematic quality to the narrative which holds it away from the specific events of 1681. Dryden tends not to show a train of recognisable political episodes; there are no parliamentary debates, no dissolutions, no trials, no murders, even though Cowley's *Davideis*, Milton's *Paradise Lost*, and Oldham's *Satyrs upon the Jesuits* would have suggested ways to handle such topics had he wished to do so.[6] Dryden prefers to concentrate upon the characters of the Whigs and (less cogently) the Tories, assuming the authorial power to reshape the identities of the leaders and to cast others into oblivion:

To speak the rest, who better are forgot,
Would tyre a well breath'd Witness of the Plot:

(ll. 630–1)

We are to understand that unlike such witnesses the narrator tells the truth. After the collection of portraits, Dryden ends his poem with David making an authoritative speech after careful reflection upon what has happened. The pronouncement is made not in any specific historical time but in a present tense which is fraught with the eternal majesty and authority of God:

With all these loads of Injuries opprest,
And long revolving, in his carefull Breast,
Th' event of things; at last his patience tir'd
Thus from his Royal Throne by Heav'n inspir'd,

The God-like *David* spoke: with awfull fear
His Train their Maker in their Master hear.

(ll. 933–8)

David foretells the fate of his opponents:

By their own arts 'tis Righteously decreed,
Those dire Artificers of Death shall bleed.
Against themselves their Witnesses will Swear,
Till Viper-like their Mother Plot they tear:
And suck for Nutriment that bloody gore
Which was their Principle of Life before . . .
Nor doubt th' event: for Factious crowds engage
In their first Onset, all their Brutal Rage; . . .
For Lawfull Pow'r is still Superiour found,
When long driven back, at length it stands the ground.

(ll. 1010–25)

The future is decreed: the rebels will destroy themselves. David
has sure command of the future tense, for his speech is grounded
in divine power and knowledge. Rebels always bow before lawful
authority – this is an established fact, told in the present tense
(ll. 1023–5). The poem's tense then shifts again for the conclusion:

He said. Th' Almighty, nodding, gave Consent;
And Peals of Thunder shook the Firmament.
Henceforth a Series of new time began,
The mighty Years in long Procession ran:
Once more the Godlike *David* was Restor'd,
And willing Nations knew their Lawfull Lord.

(ll. 1026–31)

God intervenes at this moment in history and inaugurates a new
age, perhaps even a new kind of time (as Dryden had already
claimed once before in *Astraea Redux*). But this is told in the past
tense: what starts as prophecy becomes a completed historical
narrative, and the poet consigns his characters to the eternity of a
fixed and finished story.

The individuals who are fixed into their appropriate positions in this narrative are characterised particularly through references to their physical bodies. In paying so much attention to the unruly and grotesque bodies of the Whig leaders, Dryden is implicitly contrasting them with the sacred person of the King. Conservative apologists for Charles II were redeploying the early Stuart doctrine that the person of the King was sacred, 'godlike' as Dryden calls David:

> Yes, Kings are petty Gods, who Govern men upon Earth as *Michael* and *Gabriel* Govern their Angels in Heaven, by immediate delegation from God. Their Soveraignty is an Image of his Soveraignty, their Majesty the Figure of his Majesty, and their Empire a similitude of his Empire, they are Supream on Earth as he is in Heaven.[7]

The King's sacred aura passes immediately to his successor:

> The King of *England* is Immortal; and the young *Phoenix* stays not to rise from the spicy ashes of the old one, but the Soul of Royalty by a kind of *Metempsychosis* passes immediately out of one body into another.[8]

Therefore, according to these Tory thinkers, the King is placed outside the contingencies of history in a realm of eternal stability where the hereditary succession is guaranteed by God: it is not simply that it should not be changed, it cannot be changed. One problem with this notion that the King's person is sacred and eternal was Charles' day to day sexual life, which was both promiscuous and rather public, but Dryden faces this embarrassment partly through casting Charles as David (compared with whom he is licentious but not murderous) and also by representing the King's active sexuality as an excess of patriarchal zeal, thus playfully reinforcing the official image of Charles as father of his people.[9]

Contrasted with the sacred majesty of the King's person are the unruly bodies of his unruly subjects.[10] They may claim to be serving the public interest, but they are motivated by private ends and their own physical desires. Chief among these rebellious Whigs is Shaftesbury:

Restless, unfixt in Principles and Place;
In Power unpleas'd, impatient of Disgrace.
A fiery Soul, which working out its way,
Fretted the Pigmy Body to decay:
And o'r inform'd the Tenement of Clay.
A daring Pilot in extremity;
Pleas'd with the Danger, when the Waves went high
He sought the Storms; but for a Calm unfit,
Would Steer too nigh the Sands, to boast his Wit.
Great Wits are sure to Madness near ally'd;
And thin Partitions do their Bounds divide:
Else, why should he, with Wealth and Honour blest,
Refuse his Age the needful hours of Rest?
Punish a Body which he coud not please;
Bankrupt of Life, yet Prodigal of Ease?
And all to leave, what with his Toyl he won,
To that unfeather'd, two Leg'd thing, a Son:
Got, while his Soul did hudled Notions try;
And born a shapeless Lump, like Anarchy.

(ll. 153–72)

The mind and the body sit uneasily together; the unprincipled restlessness which leads Shaftesbury to punish his body also leads him to disrupt the body politic, and the man who would produce a chaotic state by destroying the hereditary principle has already produced a mis-shapen son and heir.

In constructing this character of Shaftesbury, Dryden has taken him out of the world of history where men make political decisions and into the fixed world of typology; not granting him the individuality even of his own real name, Dryden makes all his actions the result merely of an inner turbulence; they are recounted not as elements in a political narrative but as signs of one who would endanger the ship of state by seizing the tiller. The analysis is epigrammatic, constructed out of those commonplaces which everyone would recognise, like 'Great Wits are sure to Madness near ally'd', which was passed down from Aristotle to Seneca and became a standard element in Renaissance psychology. The passage is also built up out of the common stock of contemporary pamphlets. Several writers saw the weakness of Shaftesbury's body as an emblem of his mental state:

> Double with head to tail he crawls apart,
> His body's th' emblem of his double heart.

But it is Dryden who links this image with his sickly son, and his assault on the body politic. Several writers saw Shaftesbury as an unreliable pilot:

> Like a vile sculler he abjures the realm,
> And sinks the bark 'cause he's not chief at helm; . . .
> Secure himself, he drowns the ship and crew.[11]

But it is Dryden who links this simile with his reckless love of danger and chaos. And he suggests that Shaftesbury represents in an intensified form the volatility of the mob by characterising the people through imagery of the sick body and turbulent water:

> For, as when raging Fevers boyl the Blood,
> The standing Lake soon floats into a Flood;
> And every hostile Humour, which before
> Slept quiet in its Channels, bubbles o'r:
> So, several Factions from this first Ferment,
> Work up to Foam, and threat the Government.

> (ll. 136–41)

Even in describing Shaftesbury as 'daring', Dryden is adopting and redeploying a word which Shaftesbury had used of himself.[12]

Shaftesbury was in fact intelligent, highly principled and still powerful; Oates was crafty and malicious, but his star was now declining. Dryden's character of Oates as Corah lacks the intense incisiveness of his Achitophel, but is similarly informed by a reading of scurrilous pamphlets, and likewise integrated into the design of the poem:

> Yet, *Corah*, thou shalt from Oblivion pass;
> Erect thy self thou Monumental Brass:
> High as the Serpent of thy mettall made,
> While Nations stand secure beneath thy shade.
> What tho his Birth were base, yet Comets rise
> From Earthy Vapours ere they shine in Skies.

Prodigious Actions may as well be done
By Weavers issue, as by Princes Son.

(ll. 632–9)

In the Bible the brazen serpent erected by Moses heals those who look upon it, but Oates, brazen in his shameless inventions, infects the nation. The sexual innuendo in 'erect thy self' is the closest Dryden comes to mentioning Oates' homosexuality, which was used against him by several writers:

> He seldom frequents the Company of Women, but keeps private Communication with four *Bums* ... *also* ... *with a Masculine Chamber-maid, which he keeps to scour his* Yard.

This campaigner against the hereditary royal succession is himself a self-made man, the son of a mere weaver. The same pamphleteer, with a somewhat less refined manner than Dryden, brought Oates' sexual misdemeanours, social status and nonconformist preaching together in the observation: 'He is one that preached B————y before the Weavers, in respect to his Father being one of the same Trade and Tribe'.[13] Enough had already been said along these lines for Dryden's hints to be sufficiently damning: the poem works deftly by implication, using the dirt which others had already thrown, while maintaining an ostensible decorum. The passage continues with a detailed description of Oates' countenance:

> Sunk were his Eyes, his Voyce was harsh and loud,
> Sure signs he neither Cholerick was, nor Proud:
> His long Chin prov'd his Wit; his Saintlike Grace
> A Church Vermilion, and a *Moses*'s Face;

(ll. 646–9)

Dryden was hardly exaggerating, for one who knew him said:

> Oates had an extremely stupid mind, a babbling tongue, the speech of the gutter, and a strident and sing-song voice, so that he seemed to wail rather than to speak. His memory was bad, never repeating accurately what had been said; his brow was

low, his eyes small and sunk deep in his head; his face was flat, compressed in the middle so as to look like a dish or a discus; on each side were prominent ruddy cheeks; his nose was snub, his mouth in the very centre of his face, for his chin was almost equal in size to the rest of his face. His head scarcely protruded from his body and was bowed towards his chest. The rest of his figure was equally grotesque; more like a beast's than human.[14]

It may seem a work of supererogation to exaggerate such features for satiric effect, but there were those who tried:

His marks are as followeth; The off Leg behind something shorter than the other, and cloven Foot on the nether side; His Face Rainbow-colour, and the rest of his Body black: Two slouching Ears, ready to be cropp'd the next Spring, if they do not drop off before; His Mouth is in the middle of his Face, exactly between the upper part of his Forehead and the lower part of his Chin; He hath a short Neck, which makes him defie the Pillory; A thin Chin, and somewhat sharp, bending up almost to his Nose; He hath few or no Teeth on the upper Jaw, but bites with his *Tongue*; His voice something resembles that of the *Guinney*-Pigs ... His eyes are very small, and sunk, and is suppos'd to be either thick-ey'd, or Moon-blind.[15]

More economically, Dryden uses the narrator's power of interpreting signs, so that each feature is made to signify Oates' qualities; at the same time the passage's ironic reading of these 'sure signs' points us to the appalling insecurity of Oates' own interpretations of people. Oates' anger and pride link him to the ambition and turbulence of Shaftesbury; his wit to the volatile wit of the Duke of Buckingham, who (as Zimri) was

> A man so various, that he seem'd to be
> Not one, but all Mankinds Epitome.
> Stiff in Opinions, always in the wrong;
> Was every thing by starts, and nothing long:
> But, in the course of one revolving Moon,
> Was Chymist, Fidler, States-Man, and Buffoon:
>
> (ll. 545–50)

while Oates' apparent sanctity recalls the puritanical machinations
of Slingsby Bethel:

> When two or three were gather'd to declaim
> Against the Monarch of *Jerusalem*,
> *Shimei* was always in the midst of them . . .
> If any durst his Factious Friends accuse,
> He pact a Jury of dissenting *Jews*:
> Whose fellow-feeling, in the godly Cause,
> Would free the suffring Saint from Humane Laws.

> (ll. 601–9)

Dryden is asserting his definitive control of these characters by
creating this series of interlocking, mutually echoing characterisations, and in so doing he is reclaiming command of narrative and
prophecy from Oates, who had used them to such dangerous
ends:

> His Memory, miraculously great,
> Could Plots, exceeding mans belief, repeat;
> Which, therefore cannot be accounted Lies,
> For humane Wit could never such devise.
> Some future Truths are mingled in his Book;
> But, where the witness faild, the Prophet Spoke:

> (ll. 650–5)

Dryden insists, then, that the contingencies of contemporary
history be reread through his typology, and from the proliferating
insults of the contemporary debate he selects a few significant
images which form a coherent description of a band of rebels who
are re-enacting that wilful rejection of God's wise governance into
which mankind has fallen ever since Adam.

Dryden also makes his poem travesty the political philosophy
which the Whigs had been expounding. This was characterised by
an insistence upon liberty, property and the people's right to
determine their government. *Absalom and Achitophel* counters these
positions by redescribing Whig liberty as the lawless and chaotic
license sought by the radical sects of the 1650s (in lines 51–6,
quoted earlier). Whiggism leads to savagery. If kings are only

entrusted with power by the people, rather than being given it by God, they become subject to their own subjects, and that very security of property which the Whigs demanded would be impossible: in such a society the people (here slyly redefined as 'the crowd') could make and unmake governments at will:

> Yet, if the Crowd be Judge of fit and Just,
> And Kings are onely Officers in trust . . .
> Then Kings are slaves to those whom they Command,
> And Tenants to their Peoples pleasure stand.
> Add, that the Pow'r for Property allow'd,
> Is mischeivously seated in the Crowd:
> For who can be secure of private Right,
> If Sovereign sway may be dissolv'd by might?
>
> (ll. 765–80)

Any change to an established and well-ordered state is folly; more than that, it is a transgression of God's law:

> All other Errors but disturb a State;
> But Innovation is the Blow of Fate.
> If ancient Fabricks nod, and threat to fall,
> To Patch the Flaws, and Buttress up the Wall,
> Thus far 'tis Duty; but here fix the Mark:
> For all beyond it is to touch our Ark.
> To change Foundations, cast the Frame anew,
> Is work for Rebels who base Ends pursue:
> At once Divine and Humane Laws controul;
> And mend the Parts by ruine of the Whole.
>
> (ll. 799–808)

The ancient fabric of the kingdom is securely founded upon human and divine laws. But this argument adroitly travesties the Whig case. Dryden refuses to say anything about the likely state of England under a future James II, and accuses the Whigs of merely seeking innovation. On the contrary, the Whigs would claim that they were aiming to preserve the nation's political and religious tradition against innovations which a catholic king would impose. *Absalom and Achitophel* avoids looking into the future by fixing past and present into a powerful and complex narrative of rebellion, in which King and opponents are seen as part of an eternal order where royal authority rests on divine decree, while mere malcontents repeatedly but fruitlessly rebel. Through all its rhetorical strategies, _Absalom and Achitophel_ is asserting definitive control over the representation of events. It was an assertion which many resisted.

*

Four months after the publication of _Absalom and Achitophel_ Dryden returned to the political debate with _The Medall_. Stung in part by the attacks on him which followed the earlier poem, Dryden made _The Medall_ cruder and more partisan. Once again he adapted an already existing image, in this case the medal which was struck to celebrate the _ignoramus_ verdict on Shaftesbury. But much of the rhetoric is reused from _Absalom and Achitophel_. Shaftesbury's true image is not that depicted on the medal, for his volatile shape-shifting defeats the engraver's skill. Shaftesbury is Lucifer, he is 'Vermin, wriggling in th' Usurper's Ear' (l. 31); he has no genuine voice of his own, but will say what he is paid to say:

> Bart'ring his venal wit for sums of gold
> He cast himself into the Saint-like mould;
> Groan'd, sigh'd and pray'd, while Godliness was gain;
> The lowdest Bagpipe of the squeaking Train.
> But, as 'tis hard to cheat a Juggler's Eyes,
> His open lewdness he cou'd ne'er disguise.

(ll. 32–7)

He is a 'Crooked Soul, and Serpentine in Arts' (l. 257) who has infected the body politic:

> ... the pox'd Nation feels Thee in their Brains.
> What else inspires the Tongues, and swells the Breasts
> Of all thy bellowing Renegado Priests,
> That preach up Thee for God; dispence thy Laws;
> And with thy Stumm ferment their fainting Cause?
> Fresh Fumes of Madness raise; and toile and sweat
> To make the formidable Cripple great.

(ll. 266–72)

This monstrous self-seeking Shaftesbury is associated with the monsters engendered by the wealth of London's mercantile community, which is represented as resulting from a distortion of natural processes (perhaps revealing on Dryden's part a political and social bias against mercantile rather than agricultural wealth):

> *London*, thou great *Emporium* of our Isle,
> O, thou too bounteous, thou too fruitfull *Nile*,
> How shall I praise or curse to thy desert!
> Or separate thy sound, from thy corrupted part!
> I call'd thee *Nile*; the parallel will stand:
> Thy tydes of Wealth o'rflow the fattend Land;
> Yet Monsters from thy large increase we find;
> Engender'd on the Slyme thou leav'st behind.
>
> (ll. 167–74)

The opposition will trade in human flesh, feasting on fallen ministers like the Homeric monsters who gorged on Odysseus' companions:

> Then, *Cyclop*-like in humane Flesh to deal;
> Chop up a Minister, at every meal:
>
> (ll. 226–7)

The poem ends with the claim that envisaging the future is now no difficult matter:

> Without a Vision Poets can fore-show
> What all but Fools, by common Sense may know:
>
> (ll. 287–8)

The future against which Dryden warns is one in which the poison of rebellion and nonconformity infects the nation, producing its own form of tyranny in place of the benevolent royal government which it has wrongly represented as arbitrary. The puritan minister,

> ... puft up with spiritual Pride,
> Shall on the Necks of the lewd Nobles ride:

His Brethren damn, the Civil Pow'r defy;
And parcel out Republique Prelacy.
But short shall be his Reign: his rigid Yoke
And Tyrant Pow'r will puny Sects provoke;
And Frogs and Toads, and all the Tadpole Train
Will croak to Heav'n for help, from this devouring Crane.

(ll. 298–305)

Aesop had told the story of the frogs who implored Jove to give them a king; when he responded by giving them an inert log they complained, but when he sent a crane instead they were soon devoured. This fable had been used several times in Whig poems to figure the fate of Englishmen who had implored God to send them a king again, only to find that Charles II devoured their liberties.[16] In reapplying this story, as in recasting the medal, Dryden is once again claiming to rectify a mistaken representation of the political struggle.

This vehement campaign on behalf of Stuart interests was continued by Dryden for the rest of Charles' reign. The prologues and epilogues of 1682–3 are more outspoken than those of 1680–1. His play *The Duke of Guise* was staged in 1682 but only after a four-month delay because the Lord Chamberlain thought that it reflected too sharply upon Monmouth. Once again Dryden was translating contemporary history through an illuminating mythology, this time a parallel between the Catholic League formed by the Duke of Guise in 1589 to oppose the protestant King Henri IV of France, and the Solemn League and Covenant of 1643, which aimed to promote presbyterian church government in England and Scotland. Dryden denied that there was any further parallel intended between Guise and Monmouth, but readers could judge for themselves. (Guise is assassinated.) Dryden turned to a different kind of drama when the King had finally defeated his enemies. *Albion and Albanius* (1685) deploys some of the strategies of the court masque favoured by the early Stuarts, and transforms the events of Charles II's reign into allegorical incidents.[17] The King is challenged by figures representing Democracy (which means 'mob-rule' in seventeenth-century usage), Feigned Zeal, Tyranny and Asebia ('Atheism or Ungodliness'); threatening dances are performed by sectaries, puritanical 'saints' and apprentice boys, but Charles is divinely protected from harm until Apollo summons him to his place in heaven. At the end the English monarchy has triumphed over sedition, which is transfigured into a grotesque fountain in the form of Shaftesbury:

> On the Front of the Pedestal is drawn a Man with a long, lean, pale Face, with Fiends Wings, and Snakes twisted round his Body: He is incompast by several Phanatical Rebellious Heads, who suck poyson from him, which runs out of a Tap in his Side.
>
> (xv 53)

Charles is called 'Albion': the name of the country is transferred to its ruler, so that it has no identity independent of him; he is the only possible embodiment of nationhood. But Dryden's political art could not altogether control events. Charles II died before *Albion and Albanius* could be performed, and when it was finally staged in a revised form which included Albion's ascension into heaven its run was cut short by news that Monmouth had landed with an army in the West Country. This time the contingencies of history would brook no denial.

*

The politicisation of Dryden's work – or rather, its entry into the factionalised politics of the 1680s – had a marked effect upon his own image and standing as a writer, enmeshing him in a kind of personalised controversy which was new to him. *Absalom and Achitophel* was issued anonymously, but the identity of its author was soon common knowledge. At least eight replies appeared, most of them derivative, incoherent, or both, all lacking the ingenious analytical wit of Dryden's poem. Although the issues raised by *Absalom and Achitophel*, and particularly the individual characterisations, provoked much comment, attention was also directed at the author, his reputation, motives and character. Previously the controversies in which Dryden had been embroiled were literary, and his career had hardly involved him in political debate. Now he was a target for vilification along with Charles' propaganda chief Sir Roger L'Estrange (known in the pamphlets as Towser the Bulldog). His poem on Cromwell was reprinted three times 'to shew the Loyalty and Integrity of the POET' as its new subtitle said.

The response to *The Medall* was more ferocious, fulfilling the expectation which Dryden voiced in his Preface: 'Raile at me abundantly; and, not to break a Custome, doe it without wit' (ll. 95–6). Edmund Hickeringill in *The Mushroom* (1682) – so called because it appeared overnight following the publication of *The Medall* – says that he used to enjoy reading Dryden, even finding something to amuse him in *Absalom and Achitophel; The Medall,* however, is merely a prostitution of Dryden's poetic gifts, and poor poetry to boot:

> TIME was (*John Laureat*) when *thy pretty Muse*
> (Young, *plump and Buxome*) no man would refuse
> Though thou didst *poorly Prostitute* her store,
> And for *vile-Pence* made her a *Hackney-Whore*
> Against the Laws of Art: (*Phoebus* is just!)
> Her *former Lovers* does her (*now*) disgust,
> *And I,* that once in *private* hugg'd her well,
> (Nay sometimes *smyl'd* at her *Achitophel*)
> I *daign'd to kiss her kindly,* and to greet
> Her lovely Ayres, *so charming and so sweet,*
> (Nay; be not *jealous* (*John*!) thou hast no cause,
> This was) whilst she within the modest Laws
> Of a *True Poet* kept –––– she's *nauseous* grown,
> Thou needs must *blush to own her* for thine owne
> If thou hast *any grace* ––––– she's poor and shent,
> *He's far from witty that grows Impudent.*[18]

Hickeringill may affect to respect Dryden's abilities while condemning his latest poem, but Shadwell's *The Medal of John Bayes* (1682) resorted to scandalous personal abuse.

The first allegation which Shadwell makes is that Dryden has misunderstood the true function of satire, and he invokes the example of Horace to define its true form:

> For Libel and true *Satyr* different be;
> This must have *Truth,* and *Salt,* with *Modesty.*
> Sparing the Persons, this does tax the Crimes,
> Gall's not great Men, but Vices of the Times
> With Witty and Sharp, not blunt and bitter rimes.
> Methinks the Ghost of *Horace* there I see,
> Lashing this *Cherry-cheek'd Dunce* of Fifty three;
> Who, at that age, so boldly durst profane,
> With base hir'd Libel, the free *Satyr*'s Vein.

This is retribution for *Mac Flecknoe*, an attempt to turn the tables on Dryden and to lay claim once again to classical principles. Similarly he travesties Dryden's presentation of himself as a convivial wit who is used to aristocratic company (the image which Dryden had presented in the *Essay of Dramatick Poesie* and the Preface to *The Assignation*); according to Shadwell, Dryden was awkward in society, and attempted to compensate for his lack of wit by coarseness:

> An old gelt Mastiff has more mirth than thou,
> When thou a kind of paltry Mirth would'st show
> Good humour thou so awkwardly put'st on,
> It sits like Modish Clothes upon a Clown;
> While that of Gentlemen is brisk and high,
> When Wine and Wit about the room does flie.
> Thou never mak'st, but art a standing Jest;
> Thy Mirth by foolish Bawdry is exprest;
> And so debauch'd, so fulsome, and so odd,
> As ————
> *Let's Bugger one another now by G—d.*
> (When ask'd how they should spend the Afternoon)
> This was the smart reply of the Heroick Clown.

Shadwell then proceeds through Dryden's career, step by step, vilifying his integrity at every turn, until he ends with an attempt to apply to Dryden the language of *Absalom and Achitophel*:

> Pied thing! half Wit! half Fool! and for a Knave,
> Few Men, than this, a better mixture have:
> But thou canst add to that, Coward and Slave.[19]

One reader of these verses wrote on his copy, 'Shadwell is Run Mad'.[20] But other readers no doubt relished Dryden's discomfort. It was a crude but effective way of refusing to acknowledge that urbane control over the world of literature and politics which Dryden's rhetoric had come to assert.

6
The Religious Writer
1665–87

'The Poet an Atheist exceeding Lucretius' commented one reader in the margin of his copy of *Absalom and Achitophel*.[1] It was a common charge to toss at one's political opponents, but in the case of Dryden it may also have reflected the interest in varieties of religious belief which he had shown as a dramatist. The changes in Dryden's own religious views and ecclesiastical allegiance, particularly his conversion to Rome, also prompted charges that he was merely an irreligious opportunist. Dryden's sceptical play of mind, and his delight in the exploration of diversity within what he believed to be a fundamentally unchanging human nature, led him to examine several forms of religion in his plays, while in two major poems, *Religio Laici* (1682) and *The Hind and the Panther* (1687) he explored the foundations of Christian belief. One might look almost in vain among Dryden's poems for the inner voice of the believer, or for evidence of private spiritual experience. Dryden's religious texts do not dramatise the struggles of a soul, as Donne's do, or use spiritual autobiography as a pastoral aid to teach the people, as Herbert's do. The public representation of such an interiority is not Dryden's mode. Instead he employs several kinds of dramatic and discursive rhetoric to explore the relationship of the individual believer to ecclesiastical and political authority, and to reflect upon the place which private reason and personal judgment have in matters of religious faith. These public texts scrutinise the very division between 'public' and 'private', and use rational argument to test and define the proper limits of human reason.

Dryden's early heroic plays which dramatise Aztec, Moorish and Indian cultures take an interest in the religious faith of these peoples, and where the plays stage encounters between European and non-European worlds religion is often made a focus of contention. When the predatory imperialism of Europeans comes under scrutiny, so too does the contribution which religion makes

114

to European self-confidence and self-righteousness. The meeting of different cultures allows Dryden to explore the question of the validity of Christianity: is it a definitively revealed religion compared with which all other cults and philosophies are idolatrous and vain; or is religion culturally determined? Dryden is not an enlightenment rationalist, still less is he a twentieth-century anthropologist haunted by post-imperial guilt; but his thinking does include a form of scepticism, a teasing, exploratory cast of mind, which leads him to set up some challenging debates both in his plays and in his poems.[2]

In *The Indian Emperour* the dialogue in Act I between Montezuma and the Spaniards (discussed in chapter 3) clearly reveals the collusion of religion – in this case Roman Catholicism – with raw imperialism. But this is only the prologue to a harsher language, for when in Act V Montezuma, now the Spaniards' prisoner, refuses to disclose the whereabouts of his hidden treasure, the Christian priest conveniently construes this as an act of impiety rather than of political resistance:

> How wickedly he has refus'd his wealth,
> And hid his Gold, from Christian hands, by stealth:
> Down with him, Kill him, merit Heaven thereby.

> (V ii 7–9)

Montezuma and the Indian high priest are fastened to the rack, and while they are being tortured they carry on a religious debate in rhyming couplets with the Christian priest. Montezuma is confident of his fate after death:

> ... for whensoe're I Dye,
> The Sun my Father bears my Soul on high:
> He lets me down a Beam, and mounted there,
> He draws it back, and pulls me through the Air:
> I in the Eastern parts, and rising Sky,
> You in Heaven's downfal, and the West must lye.

> (V ii 43–8)

While the two priests debate the truth of this, Montezuma speaks

about the predicament of mankind searching for some guarantee
of truth:

> In seeking happiness you both agree,
> But in the search, the paths so different be,
> That all Religions with each other Fight,
> While only one can lead us in the Right.
> But till that one hath some more certain mark,
> Poor humane kind must wander in the dark;
> And suffer pains, eternally, below,
> For that, which here, we cannot come to know.

Chr. Pr. That which we worship, and which you believe,
> From Natures common hand we both receive:
> All under various names, Adore and Love
> One power Immense, which ever rules above.
> Vice to abhor, and Virtue to pursue,
> Is both believ'd and taught by us and you:
> But here our Worship takes another way.

Mont. Where both agree 'tis there most safe to stay:
> For what's more vain then Publick Light to shun,
> And set up Tapers while we see the Sun?

Chr. Pr. Though Nature teaches whom we should Adore,
> By Heavenly Beams we still discover more.

> (V ii 53–72)

Nature provides all men with a degree of illumination, but Christianity apparently offers something more than mere reason can.
The Christian priest asks Montezuma to accept the unerring
authority of the church, but he will not believe that such infallibil-
ity is possible:

> Man and not erre! what reason can you give?

Chr. Pr. Renounce that carnal reason, and believe.

Mont. The Light of Nature should I thus betray,
> 'Twere to wink hard that I might see the day.

> (V ii 90–3)

Montezuma exemplifies the predicament of the man who tries to
understand the world, either by the use of his unaided natural

reason, as here, or through the invocation of spirits, as in an earlier scene. The Christian priest offers a final answer to Montezuma's questing mind in the form of an unerring but irrational catholicism. Neither wins the argument, either in this disputation or in the play as a whole, and an English protestant audience is unlikely to have embraced either side. But the debate which we watch here will be replayed in *Religio Laici* and *The Hind and the Panther* as Dryden keeps returning to the troubling questions of how we can have certainty in matters of religion, how we can actually know anything, and whether there is any ultimate authority upon which we can rely. Spiritual, epistemological and political questions continually lead one into another.

The debate is resumed in *Tyrannick Love*, which stages a conflict between the pagan Roman emperor Maximin and the Christian martyr St Catharine. In the Preface to the printed text Dryden defends himself against the criticism that in giving Maximin irreligious speeches he was traducing all religion; far from that, he was making his play a religious text:

> The part of *Maximin*, against which these holy Criticks so much declaim, was designed by me to set off the Character of S. *Catharine*. And those who have read the *Roman* History, may easily remember, that *Maximin* was not only a bloody Tyrant . . . but also a Persecutor of the Church . . . So whatsoever he speaks or acts in this Tragedy, is no more than a Record of his life and manners; a picture as near as I could take it, from the Original . . . *Maximin* was a Heathen, and what he speaks against Religion, is in contempt of that which he professed. He defies the Gods of *Rome*, which is no more than S. *Catharine* might with decency have done . . . have I proposed him as a pattern to be imitated, whom even for his impiety to his false Gods I have so severely punished?
>
> (x 110)

In the early scenes of the play Maximin, like Montezuma and the Indians, is anxious to see into the future, to know which times are favourable, and has recourse to conjuring astral spirits. But the words of these spirits are dubious, as a Roman officer observes:

> How doubtfully these Specters Fate foretell!
> In double sense, and twi-light truth they dwell:

> Like fawning Courtiers for success they wait,
> And then come smiling and declare for Fate.

(IV i 201–4)

Their speech is no more reliable than that of venal courtiers. Dryden does not, as might have been expected, construct a full debate between Maximin and Catharine about the truth of Christianity; rather, their conflict is seen in terms of her resistance to his attempted sexual tyranny over her. When the confrontation does come, it is largely couched in terms drawn from Lucretius. Maximin claims to have a power over his subjects which is greater than heaven's, and it is this power which gives him (and him alone) true free-will:

> I'le find that pow'r o're wills which Heav'n ne're found.
> Free will's a cheat in any one but me:
> In all but Kings 'tis willing slavery,
> An unseen Fate which forces the desire,
> The will of Puppets danc'd upon a wyre.
> A Monarch is
> The Spirit of the World in every mind;

(IV i 297–303)

But when Maximin claims a godlike status, Catharine corrects him:

> A God, indeed, after the *Roman* style,
> An Eagle mounting from a kindled Pile:
> But you may make your self a God below:
> For Kings who rule their own desires are so.
> You roam about, and never are at rest,
> By new desires, that is, new torments, still possest;
> Qualmish and loathing all you had before,
> Yet with a sickly appetite to more.
> As in a fev'rish dream you still drink on;
> And wonder why your thirst is never gone.

(IV i 380–9)

Catharine's analysis of Maximin's condition is based not upon

Christian theology and morality but on the account of the restlessness of desire which Lucretius gives in Book III of *De Rerum Natura*, which Dryden was to translate in 1685 (see chapter 7). When Maximin blames his predicament on 'those faults which Nature made' (IV i 392), Catharine retorts that he has fixed his mind on the wrong thing:

> Your mind should first the remedy begin;
> You seek without, the Cure that is within.
> The vain experiments you make each day,
> To find content, still finding it decay,
> Without attempting more, should let you see
> That you have sought it where it ne're could be.
> But when you place your joys on things above,
> You fix the wand'ring Planet of your Love:
> Thence may you see
> Poor humane kind all daz'd in open day,
> Erre after bliss, and blindly miss their way:

> (IV i 396–406)

Although Catharine's proferred remedy is devotion to the Christian God, her analysis is the Epicurean one which diagnoses a mind restlessly at strife with itself. For Epicurus, true happiness lay in the tranquillity which comes from being free from desire. Later Catharine speaks (rather like Montezuma) about the simplicity of faith which men have made over-sophisticated:

> Thus, with short Plummets Heav'ns deep will we sound,
> That vast Abyss where humane Wit is drown'd!
> In our small Skiff we must not launce too far;
> We here but Coasters, not Discov'rers are.
> Faith's necessary Rules are plain and few;
> We, many, and those needless Rules pursue:
> Faith from our hearts into our heads we drive;
> And make Religion all Contemplative.
> You, on Heav'ns will may witty glosses feign;
> But that which I must practise here, is plain:

> (IV i 544–53)

In both *The Indian Emperour* and *Tyrannick Love* we see mankind searching for knowledge of God, and for some secure knowledge of his own life and fate. Astral spirits will not disclose such secrets, but neither does Christianity automatically produce the answers. The simple outlines of faith are clear, and taught by nature, but beyond that lies a vast abyss where human reason may not venture.

Such lessons are dearly learned by the characters in *The Conquest of Granada*, several of whom assert their independence of fate and their dominance over the fickle power of Fortune. When Almanzor, the impetuous hero, learns that his beloved Almahide has just been pledged to another, he attempts to overrule fate, and to tear out the day which saw that promise made:

> Good Heav'n thy book of fate before me lay,
> But to tear out the journal of this day.
> Or, if the order of the world below
> Will not the gap of one whole day allow,
> Give me that Minute when she made her vow.
> "That Minute, ev'n the happy, from their bliss might give:
> And those who live in griefe, a shorter time would live."
> So small a link, if broke, th' eternal chain
> Would, like divided waters, joyn again.
> It wonnot be; the fugitive is gone;
> Prest by the crowd of following Minutes on:
> That precious Moment's out of Nature fled:

> (1 III i 397–408)

But whatever Fate has written can rarely even be read, never erased. Even Almanzor cannot break the constraints of time and undo the chain of causality which binds him. He repeatedly sees himself as the agent of Fortune; he seizes the opportunities which she offers, claiming 'the brave bold man is Fortunate' (1 IV ii 456), and like Fortune he confers benefits momentarily on others:

> I am your fortune; but am swift like her,
> And turn my hairy front if you defer:
> That hour when you delib'rate is too late:
> I point you the white moment of your fate . . .

This hour I fix your Crown upon your brow,
Next hour fate gives it; but I give it now.

(1 IV i 30–3, 69–70)

The ambitious and changeable Lyndaraxa also compares herself
with Fortune, with more iconographical plausibility than
Almanzor:

... like his better Fortune I'le appear:
With open Arms, loose Vayl, and flowing Hair,
Just flying forward from my rowling Sphere.

(1 III i 265–7)

She too wishes to read the future, though in her case it is in order
to know where she may place her affections with the greatest
political advantage:

O could I read the dark decrees of fate,
That I might once know whom to love or hate!
For I my self scarce my own thoughts can ghess,
So much I find 'em varied by success.

(1 IV ii 1–4)

Lyndaraxa may cast herself as Fortune, but the impersonation is
unsuccessful, whereas Almanzor is the bold but principled opportunist who (as Machiavelli had counselled) makes good use of
what time and chance bring. At the end of the play Lyndaraxa is
dead (murdered when she threatened to wreak havoc just once too
often) while Almanzor is informed of his true identity, and learns
that he has unknowingly been a Christian all along. The ending
removes him from the chances and contingencies of Fortune's
empire into the stable time-scheme of King Ferdinand's realm,
where the only problem with time is the thoroughly familiar one
that for impatient lovers it seems to drag its heels:

Move swiftly, Sun; and fly a lovers pace;
Leave weeks and moneths behind thee in thy race!

(2 V iii 339–40)

From confusion to truth; from the empire of Fortune into the realm of Providence.

*

In his work for the theatre Dryden takes the opportunity to exhibit the dialectical play between different forms of religion, to dramatise the ways in which religious belief is implicated in (sustained by and in its turn sustaining) the secular order, and to show how the religious faith of individuals may involve them in costly conflicts with those who hold political power. At the same time, characters wonder whether the unaided resources of natural reason are sufficient to disclose truth and morality, or whether some divine illumination quite distinct from the processes of the human and physical world is necessary. In these plays there is rarely a single authoritative voice, and never one which exactly represents the dramatist. Even the prefaces are carefully-crafted public texts. When Dryden turned to the writing of religious poetry he continued to avoid speaking *in propria persona*, and instead deployed a number of rhetorical strategies which promote argument and debate while rarely committing the writer to speak directly in his own voice. We do not find lyrical poetry of spiritual experience in Dryden's work, but instead texts for a world where religion is engaged in a contest for definitive interpretation, where texts are continually reinterpreted, and where such interpretation is never the innocent pursuit of truth but always implicated in struggles over political power.

Religio Laici or A Laymans Faith: A Poem was published towards the end of November 1682, a fortnight after the appearance of *The Second Part of Absalom and Achitophel* (largely by Nahum Tate); in the previous month *Mac Flecknoe* had reached print for the first time; earlier in the year there had been *The Medall* and the savage rejoinders which it drew. It was therefore not a moment when Dryden could expect to appear before the public as an uncontroversial writer on matters of religion. Religion was unavoidably a political subject. Dryden had already used charges of religious extremism when depicting Shaftesbury, Bethel and Oates; *Mac Flecknoe* had been printed as 'A Satyr upon the True-Blew-Protestant Poet, T.S.'. It is hardly surprising that the Whig Narcissus Luttrell wrote on his copy of *Religio Laici* the single word 'Atheisticall'.[3] Anyone attacking radical protestantism could be seen by Whigs as a tool of the papacy and thus a lackey of

Antichrist; besides, a deliberately careless reading of *Religio Laici* might well raise doubts about the poet's orthodoxy.

Dryden acknowledges in the Preface to *Religio Laici* that his position is not uncompromised:

> A Poem with so bold a Title, and a Name prefix'd, from which the handling of so serious a Subject wou'd not be expected, may reasonably oblige the Author, to say somewhat in defence both of himself, and of his undertaking.
>
> (ll. 1–4)

In authorising his own writing, Dryden displays a due humility about his private judgment:

> I pretend not to make my self a Judge of Faith, in others, but onely to make a Confession of my own; I lay no unhallow'd hand upon the Ark; but wait on it, with the Reverence that becomes me at a distance:
>
> (ll. 10–13)

Besides, many of the arguments in the poem are not his own but borrowed from 'the Works of our own Reverend Divines of the Church of *England*' (ll. 14–15). He has no wish to set himself up as an arbiter of faith:

> Being naturally inclin'd to Scepticism in Philosophy, I have no reason to impose my Opinions, in a Subject which is above it: but whatever they are, I submit them with all reverence to my Mother Church, accounting them no further mine, than as they are Authoriz'd, or at least, uncondemn'd by her.
>
> (ll. 22–6)

He has in fact submitted the poem to the scrutiny of 'a judicious and learned Friend, a Man indefatigably zealous in the service of the Church and State' (ll. 28–9). Dryden's stress here on authority is not incidental, for this will be one of the poem's main subjects. The Preface carefully authorises Dryden's writing through its submission to the oversight of the church (and, by implication, the state), while still allowing him independence of judgment, for when the judicious and learned friend advised him to rethink his passage on Athanasius he declined. Dryden uses the freedom which he has thus created for himself to reject the dominant creed of his youth, Calvinism, once the orthodox ideology of church and state but now increasingly the creed of the nonconformists, promising the certainties of eternal reward to God's elect who were languishing in a hostile world. Writing about the generations which preceded the Christian era, Dryden refuses to believe that 'so many Ages had been *deliver'd over* to Hell, and so many *reserv'd* for Heaven, and that the Devil had the first choice, and God the next' (ll. 52–4). Calvinism is also rejected for political reasons, since 'where-ever that Discipline was planted and embrac'd, Rebellion, Civil War and Misery attended it' (ll. 306–7).

The question of authority applies particularly to the interpretation of scripture. The Preface dissents from two prevailing attitudes, for the position which *Religio Laici* adopts – 'asserting the Scripture to be the Canon of our Faith' – will antagonise both catholics and nonconformists:

> The Papists, indeed, more directly, because they have kept the Scripture from us, what they cou'd; and have reserv'd to themselves a right of Interpreting what they have deliver'd under the pretence of Infalibility: and the Fanaticks more collaterally, because they have assum'd what amounts to an Infalibility, in the private Spirit: and have detorted those Texts of Scripture, which are not necessary to Salvation, to the damnable uses of Sedition, disturbance and destruction of the Civil Government.
>
> (ll. 147–54)

Both groups have approached the reading of scripture with dangerous notions of authority, and these have important political implications. Unlike the Whigs who feared an imminent papist coup, Dryden is clear that the greater political danger comes from the extreme protestants, whose claim to the liberty of interpretation for each individual inspires them to a chaotic revolutionary zeal. But both draw their weapons from the same armoury, while not realising that a true understanding of scripture would uphold government:

> the Scriptures, which are in themselves the greatest security of Governours, as commanding express obedience to them, are now turn'd to their destruction; and never since the Reformation

has there wanted a Text of their interpreting to authorize a Rebel.

(ll. 313–16)

Religio Laici is entering a debate in which the interpretation of scripture is unavoidably a political issue.

Much depends, therefore, on our understanding of those private faculties which we bring to the interpretation of texts. The poem opens with a passage which considers the operation of reason in religious belief:

> Dim, as the borrow'd beams of Moon and Stars
> To *lonely, weary, wandring* Travellers,
> Is *Reason* to the *Soul*: And as on high,
> Those rowling Fires *discover* but the Sky
> Not light us *here*; So *Reason's* glimmering Ray
> Was lent, not to *assure* our *doubtfull* way,
> But *guide* us upward to a *better Day*.
> And as those nightly Tapers disappear
> When Day's bright Lord ascends our Hemisphere;
> So pale grows *Reason* at *Religions* sight;
> So *dyes*, and so *dissolves* in *Supernatural Light*.

(ll. 1–10)

Here Dryden indicates that reason is not a source of illumination in spiritual matters: it has no independent status, and its light is borrowed as the light of the moon is borrowed from the sun. Reason is only useful in so far as it points the way towards a revealed religious truth. Pagan philosophers have, through the exercise of their reason, been led 'From Cause to Cause, to *Natures* secret head' (l. 13), but the identity of that first cause remains a secret from them. Different thinkers have proposed different accounts of the origin of the world or the true character of human happiness, but without the sure foundation of revealed religion, such

> ... *anxious Thoughts* in *endless Circles* roul,
> Without a *Centre* where to fix the *Soul*:

(ll. 36–7)

It is through the exercise of reason that the Deist believes he can avoid the uncertainties of such philosophical debate. Is there not a 'natural religion', a basic sense of religious devotion and obligation which all men acknowledge? In introducing such a figure in his poem, Dryden was almost ahead of his time, for deism would not begin to be a significant belief in England until the 1690s. But a few deist tracts were circulating, chiefly in manuscript, and by employing their arguments Dryden was able to define the limitations of human reason. The Deist seems to imagine a common denominator of religious experience, expressed merely in generalities:

> *God* is that *Spring* of *Good; Supreme,* and *Best;*
> *We,* made to *serve,* and in that Service *blest;*
> If so, some *Rules* of Worship must be given,
> Distributed alike to all by Heaven: . . .
> This *general Worship* is to *PRAISE,* and *PRAY:*
> One part to *borrow* Blessings, one to *pay:*
> And when frail Nature slides into *Offence,*
> The *Sacrifice* for *Crimes* is *Penitence.*
> Yet, since th' Effects of Providence, we find
> Are variously dispens'd to Humane kind . . .
> Our Reason prompts us to a *future* State:
> The *last Appeal* from *Fortune,* and from *Fate:*

> (ll. 44–59)

But even such a generalised account of what may be inferred by unaided human reason will not suffice. First, the classical philosophers such as Plato and Aristotle, Cicero and Seneca, would not have recognised such a system; besides, such notions are actually the result not of unaided reason but of revelation. They are merely the afterglow of God's revelation, 'the faint remnants or dying flames of reveal'd Religion' (Preface, ll. 68–9). So the words of the Deist are only the faintest echo of the original word of God: ''Tis *Revelation* what thou thinkst *Discourse*' (l. 71).

It is, then, the word of God which we must seek, as revealed in the Bible. But how do we know that the Bible is indeed this uniquely authoritative text? It is ancient, for 'The *World* is scarce more *Ancient* than the *Law*' (l. 135); its style is '*Majestic* and *Divine*' (l. 152); its many different writers 'weave such *agreeing Truths*'

(l. 142). Its narratives are confirmed by contemporary pagan sources, while its doctrines are authenticated by miracles, for it is through miracles that heaven enlists the aid of our senses in confirming what we read: we see the biblical teachings made manifest in creation, so that 'what is *Taught* agrees with *Natures Laws*' (l. 151). In another sense, however, the Bible goes against nature, in that it opposes our natural indulgence of the flesh, and this too confirms that it cannot be of merely human origin. At this point Dryden reintroduces his Deist, to object that this book cannot offer a general law of salvation since it was not universally available. The poet's reply assumes a compassionate God who may make charitable provision for those who have not heard of Christ:

> Who knows how far transcending Goodness can
> Extend the *Merits* of *that Son* to *Man*?
> Who knows what *Reasons* may his *Mercy* lead;

> (ll. 194–7)

Dryden returns here to the inability of reason to reach into divine matters: who knows what God may do?

So far *Religio Laici* has concentrated upon the authority of the Bible and its teachings; now Dryden turns to the problem of interpretation. He takes his cue from Richard Simon's *Critical History of the Old Testament* (1682)[4] which had recently drawn attention to the textual corruptions in the Old Testament caused by the process of transmission, and the mistakes made by various translators. As a result of this book:

> ... we may see what *Errours* have been made
> Both in the *Copiers* and *Translaters Trade*:
> How *Jewish*, *Popish*, Interests have prevail'd,
> And where *Infallibility* has *fail'd*.

> (ll. 248–51)

While Simon, a Roman Catholic priest, thought that his book weakened the basis of protestantism – since it accorded sole authority to a scripture which was now seen to be textually corrupt – Dryden makes the controversial point the other way round:

> If *written words* from time are not secur'd,
> How can we think have *oral Sounds* endur'd?
>
> (ll. 270–1)

The Council of Trent had described tradition as *non scripta* ('not written') which Dryden slyly renders here as *'oral Sounds'*.[5] Ecclesiastical authority based upon such tradition is even weaker and more vulnerable to manipulation by self-interested parties than is the text of scripture.

But the scriptural text still has to be interpreted, and without the authoritative voice of the church to guide us, how can our faith be securely grounded? Such is the catholic objection which Dryden supposes. His answer is that the text, though indeed corrupt, is sufficiently clear on all important points:

> ... the *Scriptures*, though not *every where*
> Free from corruption, or intire, or clear,
> Are uncorrupt, sufficient, clear, intire,
> In *all* things which our needfull *Faith* require.
>
> (ll. 297–300)

Most ordinary Christians (as St Catharine had suggested in *Tyrannick Love*) will make their way through life relying safely on the plain outlines of the biblical injunctions, while the learned few can devote themselves to the careful scrutiny of the text, weighing different interpretations and sifting rival authorities. These commentators (including the early church fathers) will be more reliable than the mere say-so of modern church leaders:

> Tradition *written* therefore more commends
> *Authority*, than what from *Voice* descends:
>
> (ll. 350–1)

The medieval catholic church kept the Bible away from the people, 'and none but *Priests* were *Authoriz'd* to *know*' (l. 373). The church doled out portions of the text to suit her own political and economic interests (ll. 376–9), but when the Reformation put the

Bible into the hands of the ordinary man, 'This good had full as bad a Consequence' (l. 399):

> The tender Page with horney Fists was gaul'd;
> And he was gifted most that loudest baul'd: . . .
> This was the Fruit the *private Spirit* brought;
> Occasion'd by *great Zeal*, and *little Thought*.
> While Crouds unlearn'd, with rude Devotion warm,
> About the Sacred Viands buz and swarm,
> The *Fly-blown Text* creates a *Crawling Brood*;
> And turns to *Maggots* what was meant for *Food*.
>
> (ll. 404–20)

Free interpretation is no interpretation, but only another form of self-interest; again the Bible is traded, this time by unlearned men who physically maul the text.

The only safe way is to avoid these two extremes, neither surrendering one's judgment wholly to a self-interested church, nor giving free rein to one's own self-interest. Where private judgment runs counter to the teachings of the church, however,

> That private Reason 'tis more Just to curb,
> Than by Dispute the publick Peace disturb.
> For points obscure are of small use to learn:
> But *Common quiet* is *Mankind's concern*.
>
> (ll. 447–50)

It is the Anglican church, the state church of England, which provides the necessary combination of freedom and authority. The message is at once religious and political.

Like Dryden's other recent interventions in public debate, *Religio Laici* is a text which, albeit through a rhetoric of tentativeness and modesty, seeks to foster a definitive interpretation of public affairs – in this case of the sources of authority and the process of interpretation itself. *Mac Flecknoe*, *Absalom and Achitophel* and *The Medall* had appropriated and rewritten existing mythologies; now Dryden considers the very means of interpretation as they affect the fundamental text of his culture. The quarrel over who had the authority to interpret the Bible was close to the heart of contemporary political debate. The claim of the Church of Rome to have a tradition of authoritative teaching undermined the standing not only of other religious leaders but of the English monarchy itself. The claim of the nonconformists to an inner illumination guiding the righteous set up a locus of authority in the conscience and judgment of the individual which made the power of kings and bishops secondary, even antichristian. The Church of England, reverencing both scripture and tradition, curbed the excesses of the private spirit and upheld the position of his sacred majesty Charles II. This struggle for hermeneutic control, for authority over the interpretation of politics and religion, is here pressed by Dryden to its conclusion. Exegesis is the proper work of the learned, who read minutely and attend scrupulously to the play of different commentators upon the text. The rest should be content to live good Christian lives, and accept the limitations of their own reason and judgment.

Appropriately for a work with such ambitions, *Religio Laici* shows itself to be a highly-wrought textual artifact. The Preface makes a great point of empowering the author both by displaying approval from recognised authorities and by advertising his freedom of mind: the combination of thoughtful independence and modest deference becomes exemplary. The poem itself manipulates other people's texts, using contemporary tracts to fashion the figure of the Deist who is given good but not winning arguments, and appropriating Father Simon's biblical studies to new ends. The dissenting voices are made finally to speak to the poem's own power. The very vitality of texts is brought to our attention through vivid metaphor: the damaged text of the Old Testament is like a crudely mended fence (ll. 267–9); the pages of the Bible are bruised by the calloused hands of rough readers (l. 404). The poem's own techniques are adroit and sophisticated, yet Dryden disowns artistry:

> The Expressions of a Poem, design'd purely for Instruction, ought to be Plain and Natural, and yet Majestick: for here the Poet is presum'd to be a kind of Law-giver, and those three qualities which I have nam'd are proper to the Legislative style ... A Man is to be cheated into Passion, but to be reason'd into Truth.
>
> (ll. 345–55)

Or, as he puts it more polemically at the end of the poem:

> . . . this unpolish'd, rugged Verse, I chose;
> As fittest for Discourse, and nearest Prose:
> For, while from *Sacred Truth* I do not swerve,
> *Tom Sternhold*'s, or *Tom Shadwell*'s *Rhimes* will serve.

(ll. 453–6)

Psalmodist and satirist alike are appropriated, turned merely into examples of rough versification. Radical protestants had sung Sternhold's metrical psalms on the battlefields of the civil war, while their sons had delighted in Shadwell's propaganda; but principled dissent has been turned into mere linguistic crudity: opposition voices are reduced to mere sounds.

*

Between *Religio Laici* in 1682 and *The Hind and the Panther* in 1687 comes Dryden's conversion to the Church of Rome. There are no writings from Dryden himself which mark and explain that change, or offer any account of the radical redefinition and relocation of himself which this must have entailed. As a public man, however, and one who had expressed his religious opinions openly and polemically, Dryden could not escape having his private spiritual life traduced and travestied by others, particularly since his conversion looked suspiciously opportune, coming at the beginning of the reign of England's new catholic king. John Evelyn noted in his diary on 19 January 1686:

> *Dryden* the famous play-poet & his two sons, & Mrs. *Nelle* (Misse to the late . . .) were said to go to Masse; & such purchases were no greate losse to the Church.[6]

Evelyn associates Dryden with Nell Gwyn – who is defined here simply as Charles II's mistress – and describes him with the curious designation 'play-poet', as if his poetry is not merely theatrical but also frivolous. The word 'purchases' indicates his suspicion that Dryden's conversion had been bought, a libel which several other writers made in vituperative verses.[7] It is not a charge which need concern us here: Dryden suffered for his new faith after James was deposed in 1688, and it is clear that the intellectual reasons which led him to Rome were a development of the thinking which he had pursued over the years.

Dryden published his reconsidered account of the authority of the Roman Catholic church in *The Hind and the Panther* (1687). As one would expect, its design and its rhetorical strategy evidence a commitment which manages to eschew any statement of a too directly personal kind. Its allegory, in which a hind (representing the Church of Rome) discusses theology with a panther (representing the Church of England), while sundry other emblematic beasts wander the landscape, is once again a corrective quotation of a hostile source, in this case the Exclusion Crisis pamphlet called *The Fanaticks Dream* (1680) in which a hart (Charles II) protects the sheep (Anglicans) from the attacks of a panther (the Pope).[8] As in *Absalom and Achitophel* and *Religio Laici*, the Preface concedes that the poem is entering a debate which is already polarised, and in which no fair judgment is to be looked for:

> The Nation is in too high a Ferment, for me to expect either fair War, or even so much as fair Quarter from a Reader of the opposite Party. All Men are engag'd either on this side or that: and tho' Conscience is the common *Word*, which is given by both, yet if a Writer fall among Enemies, and cannot give the Marks of *Their* Conscience, he is knock'd down before the Reasons of his own are heard. A *Preface*, therefore, which is but a bespeaking of Favour, is altogether useless. What I desire the *Reader* should know concerning me, he will find in the Body of the Poem.
>
> (ll. 1–8)

Dryden also advises his reader that in shaping the debate between the two animals (and particularly in the fables which they tell) he has:

> made use of the Common Places of *Satyr*, whether true or false, which are urg'd by the Members of the one Church against the other. At which I hope no *Reader* of either Party will be scandaliz'd; because they are not of my Invention.
>
> (ll. 102–5)

But if some of the material is thus excused by being commonplace,

Dryden alone carries responsibility for the shaping of the poem, for the disposition of the debates, and for the outcome.

Although *The Hind and the Panther* generally declines to be a work of spiritual autobiography, there is one passage near the beginning where the 'I' who speaks is not only 'the Poet' but specifically John Dryden. After some lines rebuking Socinians for not appreciating the divinity of Christ because they rely too much upon their limited human understanding:

> And natures King through natures opticks view'd.
> Revers'd they view'd him lessen'd to their eye,
> Nor in an Infant could a God descry:
>
> (Part I, ll. 57–9)

the poem exclaims against stubborn adherence to private judgment:

> What weight of antient witness can prevail
> If private reason hold the publick scale?
> But, gracious God, how well dost thou provide
> For erring judgments an unerring Guide?
> Thy throne is darkness in th' abyss of light,
> A blaze of glory that forbids the sight;
> O teach me to believe Thee thus conceal'd,
> And search no farther than thy self reveal'd;
> But her alone for my Directour take
> Whom thou hast promis'd never to forsake!
> My thoughtless youth was wing'd with vain desires,
> My manhood, long misled by wandring fires,
> Follow'd false lights; and when their glimps was gone,
> My pride struck out new sparkles of her own.
> Such was I, such by nature still I am,
> Be thine the glory, and be mine the shame.
>
> (Part I, ll. 62–77)

After this passage the 'I' drifts back into being the poetic persona, but in these lines the intimate confessional voice is unmistakable. The imagery audaciously, albeit with the humility of self-correction, reworks the opening of *Religio Laici*, as if the lesson engraved there had been imperfectly understood at the time. We do not know what Dryden meant by the 'vain desires' of his youth, or the 'wandring fires' of manhood, or the 'sparkles' subsequently struck out by pride. Speculation is fruitless, for this confessional mode still avoids detailed self-revelation, and the words have no specific reference. They exist in the public domain as a version of the ages of man, refashioning that classical topos in terms of the development of spiritual understanding. Dryden's experience is fashioned into a generally applicable example. From the errancy of the individual man trying to find his own way, we move to the unerring guide, the Church of Rome.

The early part of *The Hind and the Panther* turns back to the role of reason, the question which had dominated *Religio Laici*. Reason must be subordinate to the understanding of God which is provided by faith: if the extraordinary paradoxes of God's incarnation in Christ can be believed, then reason and the senses should follow:

> Can I believe eternal God could lye
> Disguis'd in mortal mold and infancy?
> That the great maker of the world could dye?
> And after that, trust my imperfect sense
> Which calls in question his omnipotence?
> Can I my reason to my faith compell,
> And shall my sight, and touch, and taste rebell?
> Superiour faculties are set aside,
> Shall their subservient organs be my guide?
>
> (Part I, ll. 80–8)

The evidence of the physical senses must be subordinated to the interpretation of material things which faith proposes, particularly over transubstantiation in the mass. Instead of trusting to reason, we must launch out boldly with Christ as our guide:

> If then our faith we for our guide admit,
> Vain is the farther search of humane wit,
> As when the building gains a surer stay,
> We take th' unusefull scaffolding away: . . .
> Why chuse we then like *Bilanders* to creep

Along the coast, and land in view to keep,
When safely we may launch into the deep?
In the same vessel which our Saviour bore
Himself the Pilot, let us leave the shoar,
And with a better guide a better world explore.

(Part I, ll. 122–33)

The imagery recalls that of St Catharine's speech on the same
subject. This position is offered as a state of tranquillity in which
the mind is freed from that anxiety and turbulence which both St
Catharine and Epicurus had diagnosed as man's spiritual predicament:

Rest then, my soul, from endless anguish freed;
Nor sciences thy guide, nor sense thy creed.

(Part I, ll. 146–7)

Neither 'sciences' (here meaning rational, humanistic studies) nor
the senses can be a reliable guide to knowledge of God.

As in *Religio Laici*, the rejection of any confident reliance upon
private judgment is a political as well as a religious position. *The
Hind and the Panther* warns of the combination of chaos and tyranny
which it sees resulting from the fragmentation of humanity into
warring sects. Once upon a time mankind was gentle and merciful,
ruling benevolently over the natural world. Then:

... knowledge misapply'd, misunderstood,
And pride of Empire sour'd his balmy bloud ...
Thus persecution rose ...

(Part I, ll. 276–82)

The misguided thirst for empire and knowledge leads to the worst
kind of tyranny:

Of all the tyrannies on humane kind
The worst is that which persecutes the mind.
Let us but weigh at what offence we strike,

> 'Tis but because we cannot think alike.
> In punishing of this we overthrow
> The laws of nations and of nature too.

>   (Part I, ll. 239–44)

One must admit that it is a somewhat unusual claim to make for the seventeenth-century catholic church, that it is the guardian of free thought from persecution.

But if tyranny over the freedom of the mind is to be rejected, is interpretation a free-for-all? Not so, for the sects have erred in their interpretations. The Church of England finds herself in an impossible position through attempting to conflate the contradictory doctrines of the eucharist embraced by 'her diff'ring friends':

> Where one for substance, one for sign contends,
> Their contradicting terms she strives to join,
> Sign shall be substance, substance shall be sign.

>   (Part I, ll. 411–13)

Is Christ really present in the eucharistic sacrament, or is the sacrament only a sign? The Church of England tries to have it both ways, which results in a nonsensical and self-contradictory position:

> They take the sign, and take the substance too.
> The lit'ral sense is hard to flesh and blood,
> But nonsense never can be understood,

>   (Part I, ll. 427–9)

The Church of England has generated confusion by its attempt to understand the doctrine of the eucharist both literally and symbolically; the Church of Rome insists simply on the literal meaning, which may run counter to the uninformed evidence of our senses, but succeeds in avoiding the Anglican muddle which is itself offensive to the rational mind.

The problem is obvious: without an authoritative guide there will be mere anarchy in interpretation, for

> As long as words a diff'rent sense will bear,
> And each may be his own Interpreter,
> Our ai'ry faith will no foundation find:

> (Part I, ll. 462–4)

The protestant churches have no agreed authority to guide inter-pretation (Part II, ll. 425–7). They might claim (as Dryden had done in *Religio Laici*) that the biblical text is sufficiently plain, but *The Hind and the Panther* argues that this text can never have an undisputed authority:

> The sense is intricate, 'tis onely clear
> What vowels and what consonants are there.
> Therefore 'tis plain, its meaning must be try'd
> Before some judge appointed to decide.

> (Part II, ll. 385–8)

This is not to deny that the Bible is authoritative, but to insist that it cannot speak clearly without ecclesiastical interpretation; indeed, the text is 'mute' until given voice by the church (Part II, ll. 357–60; cf. l. 203). In contrast to this disputed written text, where only the marks on the page are clear, there is an authentic tradition handed down in the church:

> But what th' Apostles their successours taught,
> They to the next, from them to us is brought,
> Th' undoubted sense which is in scripture sought.

> (Part II, ll. 361–3)

Each generation in the church follows its predecessors in an unbroken chain which goes back to the age of the apostles (Part II, ll. 216–21), and thus the church of Rome has access to the 'fountain-head' of Christianity; it does not thresh around in the 'raging' flood-waters where the protestants struggle for survival (Part II, l. 277).

Dryden has effected a crucial shift from his position in *Religio Laici*. There the biblical text was perplexed by textual errors and cruxes, yet sufficiently clear in all important respects. But now speech is privileged over writing:[9] the written text is obscure, mute even, and needs to be made to speak by the voice of the church. Authority is thus accorded not to the written word, but to that speech which voices a perfectly recollected original teaching. Jesus avoided writing his teachings, knowing that errors in transmission and tendentious commentary disfigure written texts; instead his words were handed down orally. Not even the privileged form of writing which produced the Ten Commandments was free from such distortions:

> He cou'd have writ himself, but well foresaw
> Th' event would be like that of *Moyses* law;
> Some difference wou'd arise, some doubts remain . . .
> No written laws can be so plain, so pure,
> But wit may gloss, and malice may obscure.

> (Part II, ll. 314–19)

It was only because the apostles could not preach everywhere in person that they resorted to writing, and the Pauline epistles are actually a special form of speech, 'absent sermons' (Part II, l. 340).

The speech of the Church is alone authentic, and the Hind completes her demonstration of the superiority of speech over writing by quoting the words through which Christ once claimed his divine status:

> . . . looking upward to her kindred sky.
> As once our Saviour own'd his Deity,
> Pronounc'd his words – *she whom ye seek am I.*

> (Part II, ll. 396–8)

By speaking with the very words of Christ, the Hind indicates her own authority; and that this is not a blasphemous quotation but an entirely authentic speech is made clear later when her words are accompanied by stream of light in the sky:

> Thus, while with heav'nly charity she spoke,
> A streaming blaze the silent shadows broke:

> (Part II, ll. 650–1)

The silence of the shadows, the speechlessness of the mute pages of the Bible, are filled with the authoritative speech of the Hind. Speech triumphs over writing, tradition over free interpretation, the light of heaven over the inner illumination claimed by the sects.

This irresistible authority over interpretation asserted by the Hind is mimicked by Dryden in the construction of his poem. He uses animal figures, reusing the beast fables which had already been employed by various writers during the Exclusion Crisis. Through its great antiquity and its wide popular currency, the beast fable as a genre carries with it an air of authority beyond individual poetic ingenuity. There is a special quality to the allegory in beast fables. When Lycaon in Ovid's *Metamorphoses* is transformed into a wolf for sacrilegiously attempting to kill Jupiter, and for murdering his fellow-men, the animal form into which he is translated is a revelation of the man's already wolvish inner nature:

> Howling he fled, and fain he wou'd have spoke;
> But Humane Voice, his Brutal Tongue forsook.
> About his lips, the gather'd foam he churns,
> And, breathing slaughters, still with rage he burns . . .
> His Mantle, now his Hide, with rugged hairs
> Cleaves to his back . . .
> He grows a Wolf, his hoariness remains . . .
> His jaws retain the grin, and violence of face.[10]

This is more than the literalization of a metaphor, it is a confirmation that to call Lycaon wolvish is no mere poetic conceit: it is disclosing and definitively naming the man's true nature. Similarly the animal names in *The Hind and the Panther* attempt to be definitive characterisations from which there is no escape. The Roman church is 'A milk white *Hind*, immortal and unchang'd/ . . . Without unspotted, innocent within' (Part I, ll. 1–3); the various protestant sects are tainted and rapacious animals – the Anglican panther defiled with spots; the 'bloudy *Bear*' (l. 35), the Independent; the 'bristl'd *Baptist Boar* . . . whitn'd with the foam of sanctity' (ll. 43–4); the deformed wolf of Calvinism; and others which are unfit even to be mentioned, mere half-living creatures, 'A slimy-born and sun-begotten Tribe: . . . gross, half-animated lumps' (ll. 311, 314). The poet is 'like *Adam*, naming ev'ry beast' (l. 309), and from this naming there is no appeal: 'whatsoever Adam called every living creature, that was the name thereof' (Genesis ii 19). In assuming an Adamic voice, the poet associates himself with the authoritative speech of original innocence: Adam speaking before the fall; Christ talking to the crowds and revealing his divine identity; the apostles preaching before any gospel or epistle was written down; the church speaking with the voice of unsullied oral tradition; the divinely attested speech of the Hind – all these are originary voices, and the poet in naming the animals aligns himself with this spoken authority.

The discussion between the Hind and the Panther may at first seem like a genuine dialogue between two comparable combatants, even though the Hind has better and longer arguments, but the two are not equal in status: the voice of the Hind is that of the church, which uniquely speaks the word and will of God. The Panther's voice is just the Panther's voice, and is not always to be trusted even as a true expression of her own views. Her breath may be reputedly sweet, but she often speaks with the voice of the sects rather than her own (Part II, ll. 228–30). She speaks in a 'hollow tone' (Part III, l. 56), and is reduced to silence by the Hind's contempt of worldly wealth (Part II, l. 714). Her words are evasive at crucial moments, as when she refuses to admit her motives: 'Conscience or int'rest be't, or both in one' (Part III, l. 825). The Panther attempts to tell a beast fable of her own in her tale of the swallows (the Roman Catholic laity misled by venal and self-seeking clergy), but from her lips the story lacks the authoritative cogency of the main fable. The Panther is described as 'scornfull' and 'salvage' immediately before telling this story, and the Hind in reply attributes it to 'malice' and the 'Ribbald art' cultivated by protestant controversialists (Part III, ll. 410, 422, 640–1). That is not to say that the Panther's story is altogether false: it is in many respects an accurate and plausible account of the recent history of the Roman Catholics in England, but the interpretation has no ultimate validity. It is an example of the Panther's own dictum that 'beyond the reach of wit/ Blind prophecies may have a lucky hit' (Part III, ll. 543–4), and it is countered by the Hind's own fable of the pigeons and the buzzard. This reduces the Panther to final silence, which she lamely covers up 'with affected Yawnings' (Part III, l. 1291). There is no further dialogue, only a vision of heaven which is vouchsafed to the divinely protected Hind:

> Ten thousand Angels on her slumbers waite
> With glorious Visions of her future state.
>
> (Part III, ll. 1297–8)

The poem thus concludes with the disappearance of the various oppositional voices which had been manipulated through the poet's ventriloquistic techniques. Debate ends, interpretations fade away, and we are left with one single voice, one heavenly vision.

7
The Translator
1680–1700

Much of Dryden's work was a kind of translation. His poetry often reappropriates the images through which religious and political life was currently being represented, translating individuals and causes into unexpected shapes. His literary criticism brings together writers across different times and cultures, considering one in terms of another, working out the relative characteristics of particular authors, languages and societies by a process of continual comparison. At many points in his writing Dryden appeals to classical Latin and Greek precedents, inviting us to read the present through the language of the past, and *vice versa*. That reciprocal movement through which the classics are both the standard of judgment and the object of judgment is crucial: it enables the modern writer by giving him a vocabulary of forms, tropes and *topoi*, authorising his writing by placing him in a revered tradition; at the same time it avoids disabling him by making his work merely a supplement to a structure which is already completed. Dryden's criticism moves between a sense of the eternal, fundamental stability of Nature, into which classical writers had a privileged insight, and the changing and contingent experience of human societies which gives the modern writer fresh resources and a standpoint from which to comment upon his precursors. Although this engagement with the classics always characterised his work, translation came to dominate Dryden's career after the early 1680s. In devoting himself so fully to translation, Dryden was not according to his Latin and Greek predecessors any simple and automatic authority; indeed, by the process of selection Dryden constructs his own canon from among the classics, and the very inclusion of Chaucer and Boccaccio alongside the ancients immediately refashions our sense of a classical tradition; then through the process of arrangement, by interleaving tales from Ovid and Homer with others from Chaucer and Boccaccio, he encourages us to debate the nature of authority, to ponder the play of different and often incompatible viewpoints. This extensive play between texts from different cultures raises the question of the nature of 'culture', and, indeed, the nature of 'nature'. In the Preface to *Fables Ancient and Modern* (1700) Dryden remarks (*à propos* of Chaucer's characters) that 'Mankind is ever the same, and nothing lost out of Nature, though every thing is alter'd' (ll. 448–9). Dryden's translations address the changing and unchanging nature of man, metamorphosing one text into another in order to reveal what is eternal and what is contingent in human life.

This is managed through a highly self-conscious manipulation of texts, which generally begins with a critical preface in which the modern English reader is told something about the characteristics of each classical writer. We are told about the philosophy of Lucretius and Persius, the verse forms of Horace, Ovid's obsession with witty turns of phrase and his inability to leave well alone. The translation of Juvenal and Persius is prefaced by a long *Discourse Concerning the Original and Progress of Satire*, which is not only a scholarly enquiry into the ancient origins of satire, but a critical and moral comparison of the satirical work of Juvenal, Persius and Horace. In the course of the essay Dryden moves into a discussion of heroic poetry, matching Homer and Virgil against Spenser and Milton, exploring the cultural ambitions of epic and asking whether Milton has fashioned an appropriate language. Dryden's pioneering criticism of Chaucer in the Preface to *Fables* illustrates his procedures:

> In the first place, As he is the Father of *English* Poetry, so I hold him in the same Degree of Veneration as the *Grecians* held *Homer*, or the *Romans Virgil*: He is a perpetual Fountain of good Sense; learn'd in all Sciences; and therefore speaks properly on all Subjects: As he knew what to say, so he knows also when to leave off; a Continence which is practis'd by few Writers, and scarcely by any of the Ancients, excepting *Virgil* and *Horace* ... *Chaucer* follow'd Nature every where; but was never so bold to go beyond her ... The Verse of *Chaucer*, I confess, is not Harmonious to us; but 'tis like the Eloquence of one whom *Tacitus* commends, it was *auribus istius temporis accommodata*: They who liv'd with him, and some time after him, thought it

Musical; and it continues so even in our Judgment, if compar'd
with the Numbers of *Lidgate* and *Gower* his Contemporaries.
(ll. 307–36)

In Chaucer Dryden has found the 'original' of English poetry, our
equivalent to Homer and Virgil; he can stand comparison with
those two classics, and at least in his discipline exceeds many
(particularly, by implication, the extravagant Ovid). His versification may be rough to our ears, but was acceptable in his day. All
cultures have their own form of growth towards perfection. The
manner which Dryden adopts in these critical prefaces is that of
the congenial man of letters, passing his own judgment as a
practising poet, selecting and debating learned opinions which he
has culled from the scholarly editions, and presenting a discourse
which illuminates for the ordinary reader the texts which he is
about to meet. Our sense of the literary tradition, of cultural
continuity and difference, is repeatedly refashioned.

Dryden's translations helped to mould a new readership, and
formed an important development in Restoration publishing. They
were a joint venture with Jacob Tonson, who was establishing
himself as the leading publisher of his day, issuing contemporary
writers alongside modern English classics such as Spenser and
Milton. The series began with *Ovid's Epistles* (1680), a rendering of
the *Heroides* to which Dryden contributed translations of three
poems and a preface on the theory and practice of translation.
Tonson's *Miscellany Poems* (1684) responded to and encouraged the
new fashion for verse miscellanies, where readers could find
poems of different kinds by different hands – satires, songs,
prologues, translations. This miscellany included translations by
various writers from Ovid's *Elegies*, Horace's *Odes* and Virgil's
Eclogues. Tonson's second miscellany, *Sylvae* (1685), over which
Dryden had some editorial influence, began with a preface in
which Dryden offered a critical assessment of the four writers from
whom he had translated selections: Virgil, Lucretius, Horace and
Theocritus. In the third miscellany, *Examen Poeticum* (1693),
Dryden printed substantial passages translated from Ovid's *Metamorphoses* and Homer's *Iliad*. The same year saw the publication of
a complete translation of the satires of Juvenal and Persius; Dryden
was responsible for the long prefatory essay on satire, five of
Juvenal's poems and all of Persius. Just four years later, in 1697,
Tonson published Dryden's complete translation of Virgil, the

Eclogues, Georgics and *Aeneid,* and in 1700 his *Fables Ancient and Modern,* which gathered translations from Homer, Ovid, Boccaccio and Chaucer, with some original pieces.

This sustained project derives from the cultural and commercial intuitions of Dryden and Tonson. There was clearly a readership for the Latin poets in English translation, as can be seen from the earlier success of Brome's composite Horace, and Creech's complete Lucretius. The volumes would have appealed to those who knew little or no Latin but wished to share the pleasure and instruction which these poets offered, but also to those who were concerned that English culture should match itself successfully against the classical achievement of Greece and Rome – not to mention that of France, that self-confidently classicising rival across the channel. The translation of classical poetry into English is at once an act of appropriation and humility, conquest and self-criticism. The domestication of Ovid and Virgil – with their dismemberment into anthologies – reduces their intimidating status as idols of an alien and unattainable perfection: in the idiom of Restoration translators they are given contemporary 'dress' and 'made to speak' English. At the same time they challenge English culture by forcing poets to find an English vocabulary and verse adequate to the Latin originals, and by laying English society under judgment from classical notions of culture, morality and empire. Through the domestication of classical texts, their revoicing in English, English itself acquires a different voice as images of Englishness and modernity are shaped and questioned by the models of antiquity. For Dryden it was through translation that he found a way of addressing some of the most deeply troubling issues of his life and times: human sexuality, mortality, the power and decay of empire, the place of human beings in the natural world, the role and predicament of the writer.

Dryden's translation of Virgil's *Eclogue* IX in *Miscellany Poems* speaks of the hard usage meted out to poets. Time was when Moeris had sung a song in praise of Augustus' reign:

"Why, *Daphnis,* dost thou search in old Records,
To know the seasons when the stars arise?
See *Caesars* Lamp is lighted in the Skies:
The star, whose rays the blushing grapes adorn,
And swell the kindly ripening ears of Corn.
Under this influence, graft the tender shoot;

Thy Childrens Children shall enjoy the fruit."
The rest I have forgot, for Cares and Time
Change all things, and untune my soul to rhime:
I cou'd have once sung down a Summers Sun,
But now the Chime of Poetry is done.
My voice grows hoarse; I feel the Notes decay.

(ll. 62–73, in ii 170–1)

Once the poet had urged that the old writings were superfluous,
since the present was sufficiently illuminated by Caesar's star, but
now that confident song of modernity is itself no more than a
quoted fragment from the past. The poet's voice has grown hoarse.
As the poem's headnote points out, Virgil had been in danger of
being assaulted and killed, and was forced to speak in this indirect
way (through a dialogue with an inset quotation) about his own
harsh treatment; now Dryden uses a translation of Virgil's poem to
voice, albeit through all these rhetorical disclaimers, the dangers
and the lack of reward which attend his own poetic speech.

More is at issue here than Charles II's failure to pay his laureate's
salary on time. Dryden had survived the crisis of the early 1680s
physically unscathed (apart from the Rose Alley assault), but who
knows what his public speech and its reception cost him in terms
of inward spiritual and emotional anguish? We do not know,
because Dryden chose not to use the language of public utterance –
inevitably now politicised and commercialised – to voice his inner
dialogue. He would not respond with any *apologia* to the personal
attacks on him by Shadwell and others. But somehow, in ways
which we cannot trace because they never quite emerge into the
world of writing, out of these years come *Religio Laici* and then
Dryden's conversion to Rome. As early as the Dedication to
Aureng-Zebe in 1676 Dryden had written about the self-betrayal
involved in public writing, in this case in being the Sisyphus of the
stage. In his memorial poem for John Oldham in 1684 (contemporary with *Eclogue* IX) Dryden had contemplated the premature
silencing of the poet's tongue, the young hope of Augustan
England now enveloped in gloomy night. In that poem he had
used the Virgilian episode of Nisus and Euryalus in an unexpected
way. The race in which the two friends take part ends with Nisus
stumbling and falling, while Euryalus goes on to win. In a
memorial poem one would expect Nisus to represent the fallen

Oldham, and Euryalus the surviving Dryden, left to complete the race, to finish the poetic task. But the application is reversed: Oldham is the young victor Euryalus; Dryden is the older man, Nisus, the fallen one. It is typical of Dryden's elusive mode of representing himself that this allusion teases us into a misreading, and that even when the image has been re-read against our expectations we still do not know what kind of 'fall' Dryden means. The story haunted him, for he translated from the *Aeneid* the episode of the race and the later story of the death of the two friends, and published the fragments in *Sylvae*, with many verbal echoes of the poem on Oldham. The pieces are placed at the beginning of his contributions to that collection, thus acting as a preface to all that follows.

The imaginative confrontation of death which those poems make, dramatising Dryden's own mortality while holding it at bay through translation, avoiding the trauma of writing directly about one's own death, is continued in *Sylvae* with his extracts from Lucretius. These translations, together with the pieces from Horace which follow them, amount to an attempt to work out how man can make himself free, how one may fashion a self which is not wholly in thrall to the cravings of the physical body, nor cravenly subjected to the whims of the world's political masters. It is not accidental that this struggle with the constraints which determine one's life is conducted through a wrestling with other people's philosophies and formulations: it is by moving between these different rhetorics, now appropriating them, now questioning their adequacy, that Dryden essays a kind of self-fashioning without ever wishing to commit himself publicly to speaking himself in his own voice, singly and without contradiction. In the words of Montaigne: 'If I speake diversly of my selfe it is because I look diversly upon my selfe . . . I have nothing to say entirely, simply, and with soliditie of my selfe, without confusion, disorder, blending, mingling, and in one word.'[1] Nor is the self which these translations fashion simply that of the poet: it is the reader who is invited to ponder, compare and select, fashioning his own values and mode of freedom through his consideration of Dryden's work.

The Epicurean philosophy which shaped Lucretius' poem *De Rerum Natura* ('On the Nature of Things') has often been travestied as the hedonistic pursuit of sensual pleasure, but the form of pleasure which Epicurus advocated was called by the Greeks *ataraxia*, freedom from disturbance, perfect equanimity. Dryden's selection from Lucretius identifies two of the passions which most disturb the mind: sexual desire, and the fear of death. The passage which forms *The Beginning of the Second Book* envisages a lofty stance way up on 'Vertues heights', from which the turmoils of life can be properly viewed by the serene philosopher:

> To see vain fools ambitiously contend
> For Wit and Pow'r; their lost endeavours bend
> T' outshine each other, waste their time and health,
> In search of honour, and pursuit of wealth.
> O wretched man! in what a mist of Life,
> Inclos'd with dangers and with noisie strife,
> He spends his little Span: And overfeeds
> His cramm'd desires, with more than nature needs:
> For Nature wisely stints our appetite,
> And craves no more than undisturb'd delight;
> Which minds unmix'd with cares, and fears, obtain;
> A Soul serene, a body void of pain.
> So little this corporeal frame requires;
> So bounded are our natural desires,
> That wanting all, and setting pain aside,
> With bare privation, sence is satisfi'd.

(ll. 12–27)

This 'privation' which brings content is not only the absence of wealth and luxury but an immunity from disruptive passion. Dryden's extract from Book IV, *Concerning the Nature of Love*, charts the upheavals caused by sexual desire. Love for a beautiful boy or girl 'molests' the mind (l. 19) and causes a restlessness which cannot be assuaged even by physical possession:

> For Love, and Love alone of all our joyes
> By full possession does but fan the fire,
> The more we still enjoy, the more we still desire.

(ll. 50–2)

In any case, 'possession' is a misnomer, for that very physical, material quality of the human body which attracts and pleases us prevents full satisfaction. A long and vigorous description of heterosexual intercourse and male orgasm shows how the physical body thwarts its own desire:

> When hands in hands they lock, and thighs in thighs they twine;
> Just in the raging foam of full desire,
> When both press on, both murmur, both expire,
> They gripe, they squeeze, their humid tongues they dart,
> As each wou'd force their way to t'others heart:
> In vain; they only cruze about the coast,
> For bodies cannot pierce, nor be in bodies lost:

(ll. 72–8)

Man is bound into the physical world, yet cannot bring himself to live easily with his own materiality, its dictates, its rewards and its limitations.

If man would acknowledge that he is only a physical body, he would be freed from the fear of death. After death we are simply dissolved into the constituent atoms from which we once were made, so there can be no 'we' which survives, no individual being who could be punished or rewarded. This is the argument of the extract from Book III, *Against the Fear of Death*:

> We, who are dead and gone, shall bear no part
> In all the pleasures, nor shall feel the smart,
> Which to that other Mortal shall accrew,
> Whom of our Matter Time shall mould anew.
> For backward if you look, on that long space
> Of Ages past, and view the changing face
> Of Matter, tost and variously combin'd
> In sundry shapes, 'tis easie for the mind
> From thence t' infer, that Seeds of things have been
> In the same order as they now are seen:
> Which yet our dark remembrance cannot trace,
> Because a pause of Life, a gaping space
> Has come betwixt, where memory lies dead,
> And all the wandring motions from the sence are fled.

(ll. 27–40)

Our 'dark remembrance' cannot recall our origins, neither should our fantasy invent a future for us individually after death. The mind must recognise its limitations, for not to do so causes unnecessary grief.

Why should man be so reluctant to relinquish his grasp on life? Lucretius speaks through the voice of 'Nature', who chides her offspring for their attitude:

> What dost thou mean, ungrateful wretch, thou vain,
> Thou mortal thing, thus idly to complain,
> And sigh and sob, that thou shalt be no more?
> For if thy life were pleasant heretofore,
> If all the bounteous blessings I cou'd give
> Thou hast enjoy'd, if thou hast known to live,
> And pleasure not leak'd thro' thee like a Seive,
> Why dost thou not give thanks as at a plenteous feast
> Cram'd to the throat with life, and rise and take thy rest?
> But if my blessings thou hast thrown away,
> If indigested joys pass'd thro' and wou'd not stay,
> Why dost thou wish for more to squander still?
> If Life be grown a load, a real ill,
> And I wou'd all thy cares and labours end,
> Lay down thy burden fool, and know thy friend.
> To please thee I have empti'd all my store,
> I can invent, and can supply no more;
> But run the round again, the round I ran before.

> (ll. 123–40)

There is a consolation, expressed in the eloquent rhythms of Dryden's translation, in this vision of man's identity being merely temporary, a contingent phenomenon in an eternity of rhythmic change:

> Is Nature to be blam'd if thus she chide?
> No sure; for 'tis her business to provide,
> Against this ever changing Frames decay,
> New things to come, and old to pass away.
> One Being worn, another Being makes;
> Chang'd but not lost; for Nature gives and takes:
> New Matter must be found for things to come,
> And these must waste like those, and follow Natures doom.

> All things, like thee, have time to rise and rot;
> And from each others ruin are begot;
> For life is not confin'd to him or thee;
> 'Tis giv'n to all for use; to none for Property.

(ll. 163–74)

In his Preface to *Sylvae* Dryden rejects Lucretius' thorough-going materialist philosophy, but emphatically admires the arguments of Nature 'which are strong enough to a reasonable Man, to make him less in love with Life, and consequently in less apprehensions of Death' (ll. 242–4). We as readers are invited to weigh Lucretius' case along with Dryden's poetic and critical commentary on it, testing out those voices as aids to our own self-fashioning.

The translations from Horace in the same volume consider other ways of creating a freedom. *Epode* II celebrates the joys of a simple pastoral life, where the countryman has turned his back on the turbulent world of public life with its clamorous voices:

> The clamours of contentious Law,
>   And Court and state he wisely shuns,
> Nor brib'd with hopes nor dar'd with awe
>   To servile Salutations runs: . . .
> He views his Herds in Vales afar
>   Or Sheers his overburden'd Sheep,
>   Or mead for cooling drink prepares,
>   Of Virgin honey in the Jars.
> Or in the now declining year
>   When bounteous *Autumn* rears his head,
> He joyes to pull the ripen'd Pear,
>   And clustring Grapes with purple spread.

(ll. 14–31)

Odes III xxix expresses this ideal within a philosophical context. The poem issues an invitation to 'taste the pleasures of the poor' (l. 21) and to forget the anxieties of public life, that realm in which man is a prey to Fortune:

VII

Enjoy the present smiling hour;
And put it out of Fortunes pow'r:
The tide of bus'ness, like the running stream,
　Is sometimes high, and sometimes low,
　A quiet ebb, or a tempestuous flow,
　And alwayes in extream . . .

VIII

Happy the Man, and happy he alone,
He, who can call to day his own:
He, who secure within, can say
To morrow do thy worst, for I have liv'd to day.
　Be fair, or foul, or rain, or shine,
The joys I have possest, in spight of fate are mine.
Not Heav'n it self upon the past has pow'r;
But what has been, has been, and I have had my hour.

(ll. 50–72)

Live in the present: only in this way can one cope with a world
which is dominated by Fortune – which is to say, dominated by
chance and the enslavement of oneself to the material conditions of
existence. Fortune is allegorically the fickle power who hands
mankind enticing worldly gifts but will also snatch them away
without warning: according to this viewpoint we exist not in a
providentially ordered universe where God provides appropriate
rewards and punishments, but in the realm of Fortune, whose
arbitrariness defeats our notions of justice and right, and whose
inconstancy subverts the stability of our own selves by robbing us
not only of material goods but of time and of meaning itself. All we
can 'have' is our own inner security, all we can call our own is the
present, and the past in so far as that past has been a succession of
collected, centred, truly lived moments. This non-Christian philosophy is not spoken wholly in Dryden's voice – it is manifestly a
translation from a pagan author – and yet these are Dryden's
words, Dryden's elaborations upon Horace's original, Dryden's
own eloquence. Speaking for himself in his Preface, Dryden says
that Horace's poem 'infinitely pleas'd me in the reading . . . and I
have taken some pains to make it my Master-Piece in *English*'

(ll. 379–83). Writing becomes both a challenge to the public world of public utterance, and a consolation for the private man who knows that there is no truly private life outside of political and material pressures; all achievement is predicated on contingency, and Dryden's writing acknowledges the vulnerability of all that is most valuable in the human world.

*

Whatever the spiritual questions and financial hardship which may animate the translations of 1684–5, Dryden was to face more severe trials after the revolution of 1688. The overthrow of the catholic James II by the protestant William of Orange brought an end to Dryden's post as Poet Laureate, and radically altered his role as a public writer. As a member of an opposition group whose creed was feared and whose loyalty was suspect, Dryden was always in some degree of danger. He returned to the stage to earn some money with *Don Sebastian* (1690), *Amphitryon* (1690), *King Arthur* (1691), *Cleomenes* (1692) and *Love Triumphant* (1694), and wrote a handful of poems to poetic and musical friends, but otherwise his chief energies were devoted to translation: Juvenal, Persius, Virgil and the *Fables*. Translation provided Dryden with a modest income, but also with the opportunity for a different kind of commentary upon contemporary England from the outspoken forms which he had employed under Charles II, and which were no longer safe under William III. His voice merges with (is subsumed by, but also re-emerges to dominate and supplement) the voices of the canonical classics. Through a careful selection of poems for translation, and through sly additions and asides, Dryden manages to fashion a sharp if intermittent commentary on the new order.

Dryden's Juvenal and Persius move between different kinds of commentary. The first satire concludes with the poet's advice to his muse:

> Since none the Living-Villains dare implead,
> Arraign them in the persons of the Dead.

> (ll. 257–8)

which is a clear invitation to readers to make comparisons for themselves between Romans and contemporaries. Satire III is

Juvenal's denunciation of life in the capital. This had already been translated by Oldham in 1683 and explicitly applied to the evils of modern London; Dryden keeps Rome as the setting, but takes advantage of the passages in which Juvenal voices his feeling that he no longer belongs in the metropolis; Rome is the place where Fortune

> . . . for her pleasure, can her Fools advance;
> And toss 'em topmost on the Wheel of Chance.
> What's *Rome* to me, what bus'ness have I there,
> I who can neither Lye nor falsly Swear?
>
> (ll. 73–6)

Swearing, in 1693, would include swearing allegiance to William III. Instead, says the poet,

> For want of these Town Virtues, thus, alone,
> I go conducted on my way by none:
> Like a dead Member from the Body rent;
> Maim'd and unuseful to the Government.
>
> (ll. 85–8)

The corruption, the physical and moral decay of the capital city, and its neglect of its poets, is a sufficient commentary on London without the need to name names. Even so, there is a teasing breach of this self-imposed decorum when Satire I refers to 'Such woeful stuff as I or *S————ll* write' (l. 122). Satire X, which Johnson was to translate as *The Vanity of Human Wishes*, is a more generalised philosophical poem which uses particular examples to illustrate the folly of human ambitions, and the danger of trusting our own judgments. A whole people may err, 'give our Native Rights away,/ And our Inslav'd Posterity betray' (ll. 128–9). The fate of the great Sejanus stands as an example of the transience of all political power, particularly that which depends upon the crowd:

> When the King's Trump, the Mob are for the King:
> They follow Fortune, and the Common Cry
> Is still against the Rogue Condemn'd to Dye.
>
> (ll. 113–15)

And 'few Usurpers to the Shades descend/ By a dry Death, or with a quiet End' (ll. 178–9).

The satires of Persius are rather more abstract, but still provide opportunities for political implications. The headnote to Satire IV records:

> Our Author, living in the time of *Nero*, was ... sufficiently sensible, with all Good Men, how Unskilfully he manag'd the Commonwealth: And perhaps might guess at his future Tyranny, by some Passages, during the latter part of his first five years ... 'Tis probable that he makes *Seneca* in this Satyr, sustain the Part of *Socrates*, under a borrow'd Name. And, withal, discovers some secret Vices of *Nero*, concerning his Lust, his Drunkenness and his Effeminacy, which had not yet arriv'd to publick Notice ... Covetousness was undoubtedly none of his Faults; but it is here describ'd as a Veyl cast over the True meaning of the Poet, which was to Satyrise his Prodigality, and Voluptuousness; to which he makes a transition. I find no Instance in History, of that Emperour's being a *Pathique*; tho *Persius* seems to brand him with it.

Dryden manages to remind his readers that writers in times of oppression have to use covert methods, juggling names, using one vice to stand for another. Readers in 1693 would know that five years had passed since James II was deposed; they might know the rumour that William III was homosexual. Dryden's translations teach the art of reading in a country where free expression could be dangerous, and where even silence could be construed as contempt, as it was when Dryden omitted to write a memorial poem on Queen Mary. Dryden's versions of Persius return several times to the predicament of the writer in such a society. Satire I comments on the futility of seeking one's reward in public fame, and asks only for a few intelligent and honest readers. Satire V debates freedom and slavery, rejecting the way of servility to the public –

> ... write him down a Slave, who, humbly proud,
> With Presents begs Preferments from the Crowd;
>
> (ll. 254–5)

– but also aware that man can be a prey to his own passions:

Free, what, and fetter'd with so many Chains?
But if thy Passions lord it in thy Breast,
Art thou not still a Slave, and still opprest?

(ll. 180, 187–8)

Freedom, as Dryden's translations from Lucretius and Horace had argued, may be obtained by refusing the glittering prizes of public life and retreating to a world of pastoral simplicity and a life lived close to nature, so long as man also has his own passions and desires under control. But now, in the 1690s, there is another kind of freedom which must be wrestled for, the freedom to write within a state which depends for its survival on the extirpation of those criteria of truth and authority to which Dryden adhered. To write under such a regime without subscribing to it: Dryden meets this challenge through the multiple voices of his translation, the invitations to construct parallels, and the refusal to align himself identifiably with any specific portion of the text or any particular interpretation.

Among these many daily frustrations which attended Dryden's work, one great failure remained in his memory. In classical and renaissance terms the crowning fulfilment of the poet's art was the composition of an epic. Through epic the poet spoke to his nation about its origins and its ethos; he worked up its history into a mythology; he recorded and taught virtue; the long and intricate fabric of the epic poem was his and his people's monument. Dryden had contemplated an epic, as he told the Earl of Dorset in the *Discourse Concerning Satire* prefixed to the translation of Juvenal and Persius:

I had intended ... (though far unable for the attempt of such a Poem) ... to have left the Stage, to which my Genius never much inclin'd me, for a Work which wou'd have taken up my Life in the performance of it. This too, I had intended chiefly for the Honour of my Native Country, to which a Poet is particularly oblig'd: ... But being encourag'd only with fair Words, by King *Charles* II, my little Sallary ill paid, and no prospect of a future Subsistance, I was then Discourag'd in the beginning of my Attempt; and now Age has overtaken me; and Want, a more insufferable Evil, through the Change of the Times, has wholly disenabl'd me.

(ll. 614–40)

Even if Dryden's finances had permitted, public circumstances no longer allowed him to see himself as the poet of his nation, England's Virgil. From the dream of emulating the *Aeneid* Dryden turned to the task of translating it. The *Aeneid* may be the epic of the founding of Rome, but it is also, construed another way, the story of an almost overwhelming loss: the destruction of Troy, the wanderings which Aeneas is forced to endure as a result of confusion and rivalry amongst the gods. Particularly in the early books, Dryden's translation responds to images of cities built and destroyed. Aeneas is a wanderer, exiled from the ruined city which had once seemed so strong, and not yet in possession of his promised kingdom. While this story is not an allegory of Dryden's own plight in the England of the 1690s, the translation nevertheless speaks against the glorification of English culture and history which Dryden's unwritten epic might have made. Dryden resisted pressure from Tonson to dedicate the translation to King William, which would have been the amplest possible confirmation of the usurper's rule: William as Augustus, secure in his imperial lordship over the nation and its culture. There are indeed times when omission speaks louder than words.

In Book I Aeneas views the splendid city which the Carthaginians are building, an ideal (and for the England of 1696 an ironically impossible) example of national unity in the construction of a cultural identity. Aeneas views this successful fabric with the longing eyes of an outsider, and then passing into Juno's temple he sees the tragedy of his own city commemorated in paintings around the walls:

> He stop'd, and weeping said, O Friend! ev'n here
> The Monuments of *Trojan* Woes appear!
> Our known Disasters fill ev'n foreign Lands:
> See there, where old unhappy *Priam* stands!
> Ev'n the Mute Walls relate the Warrior's Fame,
> And *Trojan* Griefs the *Tyrians* Pity claim . . .
> Elsewhere he saw where *Troilus* defy'd
> *Achilles*, and unequal Combat try'd.
> Then, where the Boy disarm'd with loosen'd Reins,
> Was by his Horses hurry'd o're the Plains:
> Hung by the Neck and Hair, and drag'd around,
> The hostile Spear yet sticking in his Wound;
> With tracks of Blood inscrib'd the dusty Ground.
>
> (ll. 644–69)

The only monuments of Troy which survive are these images of her woe, her only inscription the blood writing on the dusty ground.

In Book VI Aeneas visits the underworld, and the ghost of his father Anchises shows him the future greatness of the Roman state. The parade of heroes ends not with a vision of glory and stability, but with a troubling image of unfulfilled promise, a 'Godlike Youth' with a gloomy and dejected countenance:

> Observe the Crowds that compass him around;
> All gaze, and all admire, and raise a shouting sound:
> But hov'ring Mists around his Brows are spread,
> And Night, with sable Shades, involves his Head.
> Seek not to know (the Ghost reply'd with Tears)
> The Sorrows of thy Sons, in future Years.
> This Youth (the blissful Vision of a day)
> Shall just be shown on Earth, and snatch'd away.
> The Gods too high had rais'd the *Roman* state;
> Were but their Gifts as permanent as great . . .
> Let me with Fun'ral Flow'rs his Body strow;
> This Gift which Parents to their Children owe,
> This unavailing Gift, at least I may bestow!

(ll. 1196–226)

Into this passage Dryden gathers the vocabulary with which he had celebrated and mourned Oldham, Nisus and Euryalus. It is as if Augustan glory cannot now be celebrated without also being mourned; promise is unfulfilled, heroes fall before reaching the goal. The gods have bestowed upon the Roman empire every gift except that of permanence. Anchises' gesture of mourning can only be an 'unavailing Gift'. It was perhaps an unavailing gift which Dryden bestowed on England with the publication of his *Aeneis*.

*

An awareness of the transience of political power, and of the human price which it exacts, runs through Dryden's work from *Annus Mirabilis* to the *Aeneis*, but it is in the *Fables* that we find his most thoughtful assessment of worldly power, set in the larger context of discussions about man's place in the natural world.

After finishing Virgil, Dryden planned a translation of Homer. Though he did not live to complete the project, he did include the poignant episode of *The Last Parting of Hector and Andromache, from the Sixth Book of Homer's Ilias* in *Examen Poeticum*, and *The First Book of Homer's Ilias* in the *Fables*. Dryden's rendering of Homer is marked by a terse and forceful style which attempts to match the qualities of the Greek. The violence of Homer's world appears particularly in the way rulers exercise power. When the prophet Calchas prepares to deliver a message which he knows will be unwelcome to the Greek leader Agamemnon, he turns to Achilles and asks for his protection. In Homer:

> I shall anger a man who rules over all the Argives, and whom the Achaeans obey. For a king is mightier when he is angry at a baser man. If he swallows his wrath for one day, yet thereafter he cherishes resentment in his heart till he brings all to pass.[2]

In Dryden:

> For I shall tell ungrateful Truths, to those
> Whose boundless Pow'r of Life and Death dispose.
> And Sov'reigns ever jealous of their State,
> Forgive not those whom once they mark for Hate;
> Ev'n tho' th' Offence they seemingly digest,
> Revenge, like Embers, rak'd within their Breast,
> Bursts forth in Flames; whose unresisted Pow'r
> Will seize th' unwary Wretch and soon devour.
> Such, and no less is he, on whom depends
> The sum of Things; and whom my Tongue of force offends.

(ll. 114–23)

Dryden's Calchas stresses that he is the teller of 'ungrateful Truths', an addition which gives moral authority to the vulnerable speaker. Then Dryden turns Homer's lines about Agamemnon into a broader comment on how kings in general behave. Homer's Calchas fears the king's primitive anger, whereas Dryden's Calchas knows that kings are dangerously calculating; their power is 'boundless' and 'unresisted', words which have no equivalent in the Greek. Also without any equivalent in Homer is the violent imagery which Dryden uses in lines 119–21. Even the prophet, whose speech is privileged, lives in danger of kingly malice and retribution. Dryden could rely upon his readers to know that in the classical world the roles of the prophet and the poet were closely allied: the single Latin word *vates* was used for both.

In the subsequent exchange between Achilles and Agamemnon, Dryden stresses the greed of kings. Agamemnon insists that if he has to give up the girl whom he has obtained as part of his booty, his colleagues must compensate him. Achilles objects. His opening phrase is ironically double-tongued: 'Most glorious son of Atreus, most covetous of all men'.[3] Dryden has:

> O first in Pow'r, but passing all in Pride,
> Griping, and still tenacious of thy Hold.
>
> (ll. 183–4)

The idea of honour and nobility in Homer's *kudiste* is translated here into power and pride, while the greed is given a whole line which reduces the king to his clutching fingers. Later, Dryden's Achilles refers to Agamemnon's 'hook'd rapacious Hands' which 'usurp' the best prizes (l. 247), images which again have no equivalent in Homer.

This later speech also questions the whole object of the war against Troy. Achilles says that he has no quarrel with Priam and Paris. In Homer:

> But you, shameless one, we followed here, that you might be glad, seeking to win recompense from the Trojans for Menelaus and for yourself, dog-face.[4]

In Dryden:

> Thee, frontless Man, we follow'd from afar;
> Thy Instruments of Death, and Tools of War.
> Thine is the Triumph; ours the toil alone:
> We bear thee on our Backs, and mount thee on the Throne.
> For thee we fall in Fight; for thee redress
> Thy baffled Brother; not the Wrongs of *Greece*.
>
> (ll. 236–41)

Dryden's emphasis is on the labours of Agamemnon's colleagues who have been turned into mere objects, 'Instruments of Death, and Tools of War', and they assist Agamemnon's personal triumph by putting themselves in the posture of slaves. There is no equivalent to that emphatic line 239 in Homer, and it leads us away from the actual circumstances of the Trojan war. No one put Agamemnon on a throne through force of arms, but something very like that had happened in England in 1688.

Tyranny has many faces. In *Sigismonda and Guiscardo*, translated from Boccaccio, the clash of wills between the young widow Sigismonda and her father Tancred (who is also her king) reveals the incestuous possessiveness which he feels for her. The tale opens out into a scrutiny of the fundamental laws of human society, and raises the question of whether mankind's customs have any grounding in what we call 'nature'. When Tancred discovers Sigismonda one day making love to Guiscardo, he has the man killed. Tancred remonstrates with Sigismonda for taking as her lover a mere commoner,

> A Man so smelling of the People's Lee, . . .
> A grov'ling Insect still; and so design'd
> By Natures Hand, nor born of Noble Kind:

> (ll. 317, 321–2)

He professes to be torn by the contradictory impulses of forgiveness, as a father, and justice, as 'a Publick Parent of the State' (l. 358), though it is clear that this rhetoric of a doubly paternal care (reminiscent of the English kings' claim to be the father of their people) is a cloak to hide his own jealousy as a displaced lover.

It is the questionable status of Tancred's arguments about nature and nobility which Sigismonda exposes in her reply, an eloquent and philosophical speech of two hundred lines. First she refuses to bow to what she calls his 'pretended Justice' (l. 393), appealing beyond the rules made by kings to the fundamental laws of nature:

> State-Laws may alter: Nature's are the same;
> Those are usurp'd on helpless Woman-kind,
> Made without our Consent, and wanting Pow'r to bind.

> (ll. 418–20)

Her action in taking a mate obeys the laws of nature ('Kind'), while Tancred's objection stems from pride and mere opinion:

> Too sharply, *Tancred* , by thy Pride betray'd,
> Hast thou against the Laws of Kind inveigh'd;
> For all th' Offence is in Opinion plac'd,
> Which deems high Birth by lowly Choice debas'd:
>
> (ll. 482–5)

Guiscardo's lowly birth is an accident of Fortune, through whose activities we often see

> The Bad exalted, and the Good oppress'd;
> Permitted Laurels grace the Lawless Brow,
> Th' Unworthy rais'd, the Worthy cast below.
>
> (ll. 496–8)

So much for the legitimacy of William III. But the point is more general and more profound than a momentary allusion:

> . . . Search we the secret Springs,
> And backward trace the Principles of Things;
> There shall we find, that when the World began,
> One common Mass compos'd the Mould of Man;
> One Paste of Flesh on all Degrees bestow'd,
> And kneaded up alike with moistning Blood . . .
> Thus born alike, from Vertue first began
> The Diff'rence that distinguish'd Man from Man:
> He claim'd no Title from Descent of Blood,
> But that which made him Noble, made him Good:
>
> (ll. 499–513)

She then insists that this is a fundamental principle of nature, which mere human custom cannot abolish:

> This Law, though Custom now diverts the Course,
> As Natures Institute, is yet in force;

Uncancell'd, tho disus'd: And he whose Mind
Is Vertuous, is alone of Noble Kind.

(ll. 517–20)

If kings, through 'Pride of Mind', fail to recognise this, they are to
blame, and they have corrupted their office:

Are these the Kings intrusted by the Crowd
With Wealth, to be dispens'd for Common Good?
The People sweat not for their King's Delight,
T' enrich a Pimp, or raise a Parasite;

(ll. 551–4)

Moreover,

Ev'n mighty Monarchs oft are meanly born,
And Kings by Birth, to lowest Rank return;
All subject to the Pow'r of giddy Chance,
For Fortune can depress, or can advance:
But true Nobility, is of the Mind,
Not giv'n by Chance, and not to Chance resign'd.

(ll. 557–62)

In part this is a dismissal of any providential interpretation of the
revolution of 1688, since such things may come about by fortune
and giddy chance. More generally it is an assertion that true
nobility is independent of the vicissitudes of fortune and the
capricious tyranny of kings. Sigismonda concludes, echoing
Dryden's translation of Horace's *Odes* III xxix:

Or save, or slay us both this present Hour,
'Tis all that Fate has left within thy Pow'r.

(ll. 581–2)

Kings may hold power over life and death, but they rule by
accident of chance and through the dictates of human custom. The
virtuous and philosophical mind may see through their specious

claims and hold to the eternal laws of nature. Philosophically, Sigismonda is free; politically, however, her only free course of action is suicide.

As *Sigismonda and Guiscardo* had interrogated the legitimacy of the customs which authority chooses to represent as 'natural laws', so other poems in the *Fables* struggle to understand the place of mankind in the natural world. Myrrha, gripped by her incestuous passion for her father Cinyras, questions whether this is forbidden by natural law or merely by human convention. Dryden heightens the debate beyond the terms of Ovid's original by having Myrrha assert that incest is 'such a Crime, as all Mankind detest,/ And never lodg'd before in Humane Breast!' (ll. 37–8), while at the same time making her question the grounds for this taboo:

> But is it Sin? Or makes my Mind alone
> Th' imagin'd Sin? For Nature makes it none.

> (ll. 39–40)

This cannot be a matter of natural law, for animals are not restrained from incest:

> The Hen is free to wed the Chick she bore,
> And make a Husband, whom she hatch'd before.
> All Creatures else are of a happier Kind,
> Whom nor ill-natur'd Laws from Pleasure bind,
> Nor Thoughts of Sin disturb their Peace of mind.
> But Man, a Slave of his own making lives;
> The Fool denies himself what Nature gives:

> (ll. 47–53)

Dryden's handling of the tale (particularly his application of the language of human marriage to incest between chickens) accentuates the problems which Ovid had already set us, by leading us to ask exactly what it is which distinguishes man from the non-human world.

In his translation of Book XV of Ovid's *Metamorphoses*, called *Of the Pythagorean Philosophy*, Dryden implies that nature does indeed have laws, and that these are susceptible to discovery by human reason. Numa, the student of Pythagoras, was eager 'to learn the

Laws/ Of Nature, and explore their hidden Cause' (ll. 8–9). Man's treatment of other creatures is subject to the laws of nature: to eat animals is 'to Nature's Laws oppos'd' (l. 125), and the killing of animals can only be 'justify'd by Nature's Laws' (l. 150) if done in self-defence. Yet, while adding these points to Ovid's text, Dryden also adds that nature's laws are 'hidden' and 'mysterious' (ll. 9, 89). Our attempts to interpret nature turn out to be deeply problematic. They are subjected to a witty but still disturbing parody in *The Cock and the Fox* (from Chaucer's *The Nun's Priest's Tale*) when Chanticleer explains to Partlet that nature has arranged everything for their benefit:

> . . . See, my Dear,
> How lavish Nature has adorn'd the Year;
> How the pale Primrose, and blue Violet spring,
> And Birds essay their Throats disus'd to sing:
> All these are ours; and I with pleasure see
> Man strutting on two Legs, and aping me!
> An unfledg'd Creature, of a lumpish frame,
> Indew'd with fewer Particles of Flame:
> Our Dame sits couring o'er a Kitchin-fire,
> I draw fresh Air, and Nature's Works admire:
> And ev'n this Day, in more delight abound,
> Than since I was an Egg, I ever found.

> (ll. 455–66)

This passage confounds the comparisons and distinctions by which we seek to establish our human identity and rely upon a comically inept anthropocentric view of the world. A cock speaking human language says that nature has arranged everything (including birdsong) for his benefit; man is but a poor imitation of the birds – which is itself a definition borrowed from Plato. Through this play of different voices and viewpoints Dryden's texts teasingly upset our complacent notions of a stable human identity.

In *Palamon and Arcite* (from Chaucer's *The Knight's Tale*) the protagonists are caught up in disputes between the gods, and fall victim to the machinations of Saturn. He is master of unpleasant chance and disruption. While Chaucer's Saturn is responsible for 'the murmure and the cherles rebellyng', Dryden's says:

> When Churls rebel against their Native Prince,
> I arm their Hands, and furnish the Pretence;
> And housing in the Lion's hateful Sign,
> Bought Senates, and deserting Troops are mine.

> (Book III, ll. 408–11)

This is more than a political jibe: it associates the revolution of 1688 with the chaotic counter-empire of Saturn (alias Fortune), which also includes diseases, added here by Dryden to Chaucer's list of disasters:

> Cold shivering Agues, melancholy Care,
> And bitter blasting Winds, and poison'd Air,
> Are mine, and wilful Death, resulting from Despair.

> (Book III, ll. 403–5)

Disorders of the body, of the soul and of the state are brought together, seen as part of the same chaos and attributed in mythological terms to an arbitrary power. Political tyranny and arbitrary violence are seen philosophically as part of the way the world is.

It is Theseus who tries to work out how to understand and how to live morally within such a world. There is, he claims, an ultimate harmony in the world behind its transitory physical forms:

> The Cause and Spring of Motion, from above
> Hung down on Earth the Golden Chain of Love:
> Great was th' Effect, and high was his Intent,
> When Peace among the jarring Seeds he sent.
> Fire, Flood, and Earth, and Air by this were bound,
> And Love, the common Link, the new Creation crown'd.
> The Chain still holds; for though the Forms decay,
> Eternal Matter never wears away:

> (Book III, ll. 1024–31)

Mankind belongs within this scheme, but is subject to time and decay:

Then since those Forms begin, and have their End,
On some unalter'd Cause they sure depend:
Parts of the Whole are we; but God the Whole;
Who gives us Life, and animating Soul.
For Nature cannot from a Part derive
That Being, which the Whole can only give:
He perfect, stable; but imperfect We,
Subject to change, and diff'rent in Degree.

(Book III, ll. 1040–7)

Theseus then offers a vision of the origins and growth of man:

So Man, at first a Drop, dilates with Heat,
Then form'd, the little Heart begins to beat;
Secret he feeds, unknowing in the Cell;
At length, for Hatching ripe, he breaks the Shell,
And struggles into Breath, and cries for Aid;
Then, helpless, in his Mothers Lap is laid.
He creeps, he walks, and issuing into Man,
Grudges their Life, from whence his own began.
Retchless of Laws, affects to rule alone,
Anxious to reign, and restless on the Throne:
First vegetive, then feels, and reasons last;
Rich of Three Souls, and lives all three to waste.

(Book III, ll. 1066–77)

At first there is nothing to distinguish man from inanimate matter:
he is just a 'Drop'; he remains unconscious, 'unknowing'. When he
is ready to be born he is ripe like a fruit, and hatches from his shell
like a bird. We are left pondering the mystery of rational man in a
material universe.

Theseus' conclusion urges acceptance and self-possession:

What then remains, but after past Annoy,
To take the good Vicissitude of Joy?
To thank the gracious Gods for what they give,
Possess our Souls, and while we live, to live?

(Book III, ll. 1111–14)

Theseus' speech has a special eloquence. It recognises the mutability of all human fabrics, and searches for a gentle, centred humanity in a world which may ultimately be sustained by love, but which often turns towards us a face of violent change. It is one of Dryden's most attractive voices. But to end an account of Dryden's career on that note would be an arbitrary device. Theseus' is only one of the voices in the *Fables*. There is no last word, no privileged viewpoint. The collection is an anthology of many contrasting and conflicting voices, and the volume actually ends by reprinting the original texts of the Chaucerian poems which Dryden translates. It is a gesture which invites the reader into the work of comparison and interpretation, into the continual movement from text to text.

Epilogue

There is some evidence to suggest that the confident command of rhetoric and multiple voices which Dryden's writing displayed did not come easily to him in daily social life. Shadwell's *The Medal of John Bayes* (quoted in chapter 5) asserts that Dryden's social embarrassment led him to produce crude obscenity which he mistook for wit. Whether true or not, such an appropriation of Dryden's voice and representation of his intimate discourse with friends is an instance of the continual traducing and translation which Dryden suffered at the hands of his enemies. But there are other interpretations of Dryden's convivial manner; one W.G. recalled:

> Posterity is absolutely mistaken as to that great man; tho' forced to be a satirist, he was the mildest creature breathing, and the readiest to help the young and deserving ... He was in company the modestest man that ever convers'd ... *Shadwell* in conversation was a brute.[1]

And William Congreve wrote warmly about his friend:

> He was of a Nature exceedingly Humane and Compassionate; easily forgiving Injuries, and capable of a prompt and sincere Reconciliation with them who had offended him ... As his Reading had been very extensive, so was he very happy in a Memory tenacious of every thing that he had read. He was not more possess'd of Knowledge than he was Communicative of it. But then his Communication of it was by no means pedantick, or impos'd upon the Conversation ... He was of very easy, I may say of very pleasing Access: But something slow, and as it were diffident in his Advances to others. He had something in his Nature that abhorr'd Intrusion into any Society whatsoever ... by that means, he was Personally less known, and consequently his Character might become liable both to Misapprehensions and Misrepresentations ... he was, of all the Men that ever I knew, one of the most Modest, and the most Easily to be discountenanced, in his Approaches, either to his Superiors, or his Equals.[2]

Such quotations can only be gestures towards commemorating the valued friend, the modest and genial private man, and ensuring that his image is not wholly within the control of malicious opponents. For us, only the writings remain, but these writings enact a struggle for integrity in a world where violent change seemed to threaten every kind of stability which made life intelligible. Dryden's work advocates a settled and stable political order, while aware of the hypocrisy of imperialism and the tyranny into which government so easily degenerates; it explores the need which man has to comprehend himself, his passions and his fears, and shows the difficulty of knowing one's identity and interpreting one's place in a universe whose ways can be explained by so many contradictory mythologies. Writing which once sought to shape a cultured and humane establishment found itself confronting the failure of those hopes, and Dryden was forced to speak from within a reviled and feared minority. For any who share such a position, for any who understand such a combination of commitment and scepticism, belonging and alienation, Dryden's work offers a testimony that it is still possible to fashion an integrity and a freedom by resisting the representations which others make of you, and using all the rhetorical resources of play, parody, translation, multiple voices and covert allusion to undo the tyranny of language: thus by many fictions to speak clear and free.

Select Bibliography

The place of publication is London unless stated otherwise.

Dryden's Works

The Poems of John Dryden, edited by James Kinsley, 4 vols (Oxford, 1958). Unless otherwise stated, quotations from Dryden's poems and their prefaces are taken from this edition, with references by line numbers.

The Works of John Dryden, edited by H. T. Swedenberg et al., 20 vols (Berkeley, 1956–), in progress. Quotations from Dryden's plays and prose works are taken from this edition where available; references are by volume and page number.

Of Dramatic Poesy and other critical essays, edited by George Watson, 2 vols (1962).

The Letters of John Dryden, edited by Charles E. Ward (Durham, NC, 1942).

Bibliographical Works

Hugh Macdonald, *John Dryden: A Bibliography of Early Editions and of Drydeniana* (Oxford, 1939). This was corrected and supplemented by James M. Osborn in *Modern Philology* 39 (1941) 69–98, 197–212.

Peter Beal, *Index of English Literary Manuscripts*, vol. 2, part 1 (1987) pp. 383–428. Lists manuscript copies of Dryden's works.

David J. Latt and Samuel Holt Monk, *John Dryden: A Survey and Bibliography of Critical Studies, 1895–1974* (Minneapolis, 1976). Subsequent studies are listed in various periodicals, including *Restoration, The Scriblerian* and *The Year's Work in English Studies*.

Biographical Works

Samuel Johnson, *Lives of the English Poets*, edited by George Birkbeck Hill, vol. 1 (Oxford, 1905) pp. 331–487.

Hugh Macdonald, 'The Attacks on Dryden', *Essays and Studies* 21 (1936) 41–74.

James M. Osborn, *John Dryden: Some Biographical Facts and Problems*, revised edition (Gainesville, 1965).

James Anderson Winn, *John Dryden and his World* (New Haven, 1987). This fine biography provides detailed information on many of the topics discussed in the present book. For reasons of economy, repeated cross-references to Winn's book are not given in the notes which follow.

Criticism

Studies of particular areas of Dryden's work are cited in the headnote to each chapter, but several general studies deserve notice:

Louis I. Bredvold, *The Intellectual Milieu of John Dryden* (Ann Arbor, 1924). Supplemented but not altogether replaced by Harth (see headnote to ch. 6).
James D. Garrison, *Dryden and the Tradition of Panegyric* (Berkeley, 1975).
Arthur W. Hoffman, *John Dryden's Imagery* (Gainesville, 1962).
David Hopkins, *John Dryden* (Cambridge, 1986).
James and Helen Kinsley (eds), *Dryden: The Critical Heritage* (1971).
George McFadden, *Dryden the Public Writer 1660–1685* (Princeton, 1978).
Earl Miner, *Dryden's Poetry* (Bloomington, 1967).
Earl Miner (ed), *John Dryden* (1972). A collection of essays.
Mark Van Doren, *John Dryden: A Study of his Poetry* (Bloomington, 1920; revised 1946).
Steven N. Zwicker, *Dryden's Political Poetry: The Typology of King and Nation* (Providence, 1972).
Steven N. Zwicker, *Politics and Language in Dryden's Poetry: The Arts of Disguise* (Princeton, 1984).

Dryden's Cultural and Political World

Only a few preliminary suggestions can be offered in this field. The best general account of the Restoration period is still David Ogg, *England in the Reign of Charles II* (Oxford, 1934). Two recent books by Ronald Hutton are very useful: *The Restoration: A Political and Religious History of England and Wales 1658–1667* (Oxford, 1985), and his biography *Charles the Second: King of England, Scotland, and Ireland* (Oxford, 1989). *The Diary of Samuel Pepys*, edited by Robert Latham and William Matthews, 11 vols (1970–83) is an invaluable source for the earlier part of Charles' reign. *Poems on Affairs of State*, edited by George deF. Lord et al., 7 vols (New Haven, 1963–75) collects many samples of the public poetry of the age.

Notes

Prologue

1. *The Essays of Michael, Lord of Montaigne,* translated by John Florio, 3 vols (1904–6) ii 6–7.

Chapter 1

Dryden's education would initially have been shaped by the puritan attitudes prevailing in his family, which are well discussed by Winn, pp. 1–35; for the general context see John Morgan, *Godly Learning: Puritan Attitudes towards Reason, Learning, and Education, 1560–1640* (Cambridge, 1986). Details of the Westminster curriculum are given by Winn, pp. 521–4. For Dryden at Cambridge see Paul Hammond, 'Dryden and Trinity', *Review of English Studies* 36 (1985) 35–57.

1. Abraham Cowley, *Poems,* edited by A. R. Waller (Cambridge, 1905) p. 7.
2. Paul Hammond, 'The Integrity of Dryden's Lucretius', *Modern Language Review* 78 (1983) 1–23, p. 12.
3. 'I remember, when I was a boy, I thought Spenser a mean poet in comparison of Sylvester's *Dubartas*' (*Of Dramatic Poesy,* ed. Watson, i 277).
4. 'For *witness* is a Common Name to all' (*Absalom and Achitophel,* l. 618) is an adaptation of '*Homo,* is a commune name to all men' from William Lily and John Colet's *A Shorte Introduction of Grammar* (1549) p. 7.
5. Headnote to 'The Third Satyr' of Persius.
6. Paul Hammond, 'Dryden's Zimri and Juvenal', *Notes and Queries* 223 (1978) 26; Paul Hammond, review in *Review of English Studies* 33 (1982) 326.
7. 'Of English Verse', ll. 13–16; in *The Poems of Edmund Waller,* edited by G. Thorn Drury, 2 vols (1901).
8. Michael Gearin-Tosh, 'Marvell's "Upon the Death of the Lord Hastings"', *Essays and Studies* 34 (1981) 105–22.
9. John Templer, *The Saints Duty in contending for the Faith delivered to them* (1659) p. 15; *A Treatise relating to the Worship of God* (1694) p. 107.
10. James Bass Mullinger, *The University of Cambridge,* vol. 3 (Cambridge, 1911) p. 271.
11. *The Theological Works of Isaac Barrow, D.D.,* edited by Alexander Napier, vol. 9 (Cambridge, 1859) p. viii.
12. 'To goodman Page for carving the States armes over the new court gate and takeing downe ye Kings £3-17s-0d'; 'To John Woodruffe for carving the States arms and setting them up in the Hall £7-0-0'

(Trinity College Muniments, 'Senior Bursar's Audit Book', 1651). Quotations from the Trinity College muniments and manuscripts are made by kind permission of the Master and Fellows.

13. *Dictionary of National Biography*, Hill.
14. Duport's rules are quoted from the copy in Trinity College Library, MS 0.10A.33; there is a more complete copy in Cambridge University Library, MS Add 6986.
15. Trinity College Muniments, 'Conclusions and Admonitions 1607–73', p. 221.
16. Thomas Shadwell, *The Medal of John Bayes* (1682) p. 8.
17. *The Historical Register of the University of Cambridge*, edited by J. R. Tanner (Cambridge, 1917) p. 407; Trinity College Muniments, 'Conclusions and Admonitions 1607–1673', p. 237.
18. Samuel Johnson, *Lives*, p. 334.
19. 'A Turncoat of the Times', ll. 10–18, 82–90, in *The Roxburghe Ballads*, edited by J. W. Ebsworth, vol. 4 (Hertford, 1883) pp. 517–19.
20. Samuel Pordage, *The Medal Revers'd* (1682) pp. 1–2.
21. *Dictionary of National Biography*, Pickering; Austin Woolrych, *Commonwealth to Protectorate* (Oxford, 1982) p. 200; *Calendar of State Papers Domestic 1655–56*, pp. 20, 218; *CSPD 1655–57*, p. 355.
22. Shadwell, p. 8.
23. Public Record Office SP 18/180/95; Paul Hammond, 'Dryden's Employment by Cromwell's Government', *Transactions of the Cambridge Bibliographical Society* 8 (1981) 130–6.
24. Bodleian Library Oxford, MS Rawlinson A 38 f.260^r.
25. British Library MS Lansdowne 95 f.41^v.
26. Paul Hammond, 'Dryden's use of Marvell's *Horatian Ode* in *Absalom and Achitophel*', *Notes and Queries* 233 (1988) 173–4.
27. For illustrations see Antonia Fraser, *Cromwell our chief of men* (1973) opposite pp. 285, 476, 700.
28. Machiavelli, *The Prince*, translated by Edward Dacres (1640), Tudor Translations Series 39 (1905), p. 352.

Chapter 2

For the imagery of *Astraea Redux* see H. T. Swedenberg, 'England's Joy: *Astraea Redux* in its setting', *Studies in Philology* 50 (1953) 30–44, and Howard Erskine-Hill, *The Augustan Idea in English Literature* (1983) pp. 213–22. The context of *Annus Mirabilis* is well described by Michael McKeon in his *Politics and Poetry in Restoration England: The Case of Dryden's 'Annus Mirabilis'* (Cambridge, Mass., 1975). The account of *Annus Mirabilis* given in the present chapter is elaborated in my 'John Dryden: The Classicist as Sceptic', *The Seventeenth Century*, 4 (1989) 165–87. For alternative readings see Miner (1967) pp. 3–35, and Michael G. Ketcham, 'Myth and Anti-Myth and the Poetics of Political Events in Two Restoration Poems', *Studies in Eighteenth-Century Culture* 13 (1984) 117–32. On Restoration science see Michael Hunter, *Science and Society in Restoration England* (Cambridge, 1981) and *Establishing the New Science: The Experience of the Early Royal Society* (Woodbridge, 1989).

1. Winn, p. 123.
2. Fortune is prominent in *Annus Mirabilis*; see also Paul Hammond, 'Dryden's Philosophy of Fortune', *Modern Language Review* 80 (1985) 769–85.
3. As David M. Vieth argues, 'Irony in Dryden's Verses to Sir Robert Howard', *Essays in Criticism* 22 (1972) 239–43.
4. See Garrison, *passim*.
5. Thomas Hobbes, *Leviathan*, edited by C. B. Macpherson (Harmondsworth, 1968) p. 120.
6. Dryden's translation of the *Aeneid*, Book II l. 763; verbatim from Sir John Denham's translation.
7. Pepys, *Diary* vii 207.
8. Dryden drew particularly upon several numbers of *The London Gazette* and the official pamphlet *A True Narrative of the Engagement* (1666).
9. René Le Bossu, *Traité du Poème Épique* (1675).
10. *The London Gazette* 85 (3–10 September, 1666).
11. Trinity College Library, Cambridge, H.24.56.
12. See Douglas Jefferson, 'Aspects of Dryden's Imagery', *Essays in Criticism* 4 (1954) 20–41; and Harold Love, 'Dryden's "Unideal Vacancy"', *Eighteenth-Century Studies* 12 (1978) 74–89 and 'Dryden's Rationale of Paradox', *ELH* 51 (1984) 297–313.
13. Thomas Sprat, *The History of the Royal-Society of London, For the Improving of Natural Knowledge* (1667) p. 362.
14. Roland Barthes, *Mythologies*, selected and translated by Annette Lavers (1973) p. 155.

Chapter 3

An essential reference work is *The London Stage 1660–1800*, Part I: 1660–1700, edited by William Van Lennep (Carbondale, 1965), which provides a calendar of performances (now in need of revision) and a valuable introductory essay by Emmett L. Avery and Arthur H. Scouten on all aspects of the Restoration theatre. The physical form of the playhouses is well discussed by Richard Leacroft in *The Development of the English Playhouse* (1973, revised 1988). Harold Love has an important article on 'Who were the Restoration Audience?' in *Yearbook of English Studies* 10 (1980) 21–44. A masterly account of Restoration drama is provided by Robert D. Hume in *The Development of English Drama in the Late Seventeenth Century* (Oxford, 1976), while Jocelyn Powell's *Restoration Theatre Production* (1984) discusses styles of acting and production. Susan Staves' *Players' Scepters: Fictions of Authority in the Restoration* (Lincoln, Nebraska, 1979) uses the drama as part of a wide-ranging argument about authority in Restoration society. There are several useful books on Dryden's drama: Eugene M. Waith, *The Herculean Hero* (1962) pp. 152–201; Arthur C. Kirsch, *Dryden's Heroic Drama* (Princeton, 1965); Anne T. Barbeau, *The Intellectual Design of John Dryden's Heroic Plays* (New Haven, 1970); and, particularly, Derek Hughes, *Dryden's Heroic Plays* (1981), to which this chapter is specially indebted. Two articles relevant to the material in this chapter are

Michael West, 'Dryden and the Disintegration of Renaissance Heroic Ideals', *Costerus* 7 (1973) 193–222, and J. M. Armistead, 'The Occultism of Dryden's "American" Plays in Context', *The Seventeenth Century* 1 (1986) 127–52.

1. Leacroft, p. 82; Pepys vii 76.
2. Dryden, 'A Prologue spoken at the Opening of the New House, Mar. 26. 1674', l. 1.
3. See Love.
4. The dates in this paragraph are of first performance, some of them conjectural.
5. Pepys iv 56.
6. Pepys ix 248.
7. See Powell.
8. See Hughes for an extensive discussion of this.
9. Shakespeare, *Troilus and Cressida* III ii 81–2.
10. On Dryden's interest in the sexual behaviour of other societies see Maximillian E. Novak's notes to *The Tempest* in *Works* x.
11. *The Essayes of Michael Lord of Montaigne*, translated by John Florio, 3 vols (1904–6) iii 75.
12. Quotations are from John Dryden, *Aureng-Zebe*, edited by Frederick M. Link (1972).
13. For a wider discussion of the political implications of Charles' sexuality see my 'The King's Two Bodies: Representations of Charles II', in *Culture, Politics and Society in Britain, 1660–1800*, edited by Jeremy Black and Jeremy Gregory, forthcoming.
14. This is the first usage of the phrase 'the noble savage' known to the *OED*.

Chapter 4

Dryden's critical writings have been discussed by Robert D. Hume, *Dryden's Criticism* (Ithaca, 1970) and Edward Pechter, *Dryden's Classical Theory of Literature* (Cambridge, 1975). Hoyt Trowbridge has an article on 'The Place of the Rules in Dryden's Criticism' in *Modern Philology* 44 (1946–7) 84–96. John M. Aden studies 'Dryden and the Imagination: The First Phase', in *Publications of the Modern Language Association of America* 74 (1959) 28–40, which is followed by Robert D. Hume's 'Dryden on Creation: "Imagination" in the Later Criticism' in *Review of English Studies* 21 (1970) 295–314. Barbara M. H. Strang writes on 'Dryden's Innovations in Critical Vocabulary' in *Durham University Journal* 51 (1958–9) 114–23. The documents in the debate between Dryden and Shadwell are collected in *Dryden and Shadwell*, edited by Richard L. Oden (Delmar, 1977). For *Mac Flecknoe* see Ian Donaldson, 'Fathers and Sons: Jonson, Dryden and *Mac Flecknoe*', *Southern Review* 18 (1985) 314–27, and Paul Hammond, 'Flecknoe and *Mac Flecknoe*', *Essays in Criticism* 35 (1985) 315–29. For Roscommon see Carl Niemeyer, 'The Earl of Roscommon's Academy', *Modern Language Notes* 49 (1934) 432–7. Dryden's poem to Maidwell was first printed by John Barnard and Paul Hammond in 'Dryden and a poem for Lewis Maidwell',

TLS 25 May 1984, p. 586; see also G. J. Clingham, 'Dryden's New Poem', *Essays in Criticism* 35 (1985) 281–93. For Oldham see Dustin Griffin, 'Dryden's "Oldham" and the Perils of Writing', *Modern Language Quarterly* 37 (1976) 133–50, and Paul Hammond, *John Oldham and the Renewal of Classical Culture* (Cambridge, 1983).

1. See further Christopher Ricks, 'Allusion: the poet as heir' in *Studies in the Eighteenth Century III*, edited by R. F. Brissenden and J. C. Eade (Toronto, 1976) pp. 209–40; and, more generally, W. Jackson Bate, *The Burden of the Past and the English Poet* (1970), and Harold Bloom, *The Anxiety of Influence* (New York, 1973).

2. See Kirsti Simonsuuri, *Homer's Original Genius* (Cambridge, 1979).

3. 'Epilogue to *2 Conquest of Granada*' (1672), ll. 1–5, 21–4. This caused enough outrage for Dryden to compose a *Defence of the Epilogue* in which he analysed examples of Jonson's failings (xi 203–18).

4. The attacks on Dryden are catalogued in Macdonald's bibliography and discussed in his article (see *Select Bibliography*).

5. 'Discoveries', in *Ben Jonson*, edited by C. H. Herford, Percy and Evelyn Simpson, 11 vols (Oxford, 1925–52) viii 567.

6. But see Trowbridge's discussion of rules in Dryden's criticism.

7. Thomas Shadwell, *The Humorists* (1671), second, unsigned page of the Preface.

8. 'To utter words at once both pleasing and helpful to life' (Horace, *Ars Poetica*, l. 334); Thomas Shadwell, *The Royal Shepherdess* (1669) A2^v–A3^r.

9. Thomas Shadwell, *The Sullen Lovers* (1668) a2^{r-v}.

10. *The Humorists*, a2^v.

11. Thomas Shadwell, *The Virtuoso* (1676) A2^v.

12. For the date and immediate circumstances of the composition of *Mac Flecknoe* see David M. Vieth, 'The Discovery of the Date of *Mac Flecknoe*', in *Evidence in Literary Scholarship*, edited by René Wellek and Alvaro Ribiero (Oxford, 1979) pp. 63–87.

13. See Gillespie (cited in headnote to ch. 7).

14. Quoted from Barnard and Hammond.

15. This is surmise: it is thought that the attack on Dryden in Rose Alley on 18 December 1679 was instigated by someone offended by the *Essay upon Satire* who attributed it to Dryden (see *Poems on Affairs of State* i 396–413). It is doubtful whether Dryden had any hand in the poem.

16. See the notes in x 398–411, and Paul Hammond, 'Two Echoes of Rochester's *A Satire Against Reason and Mankind* in Dryden', *Notes and Queries* 233 (1988) 170–1.

17. John Dryden, *Aureng-Zebe*, edited by Frederick M. Link (1972) pp. 7–9.

18. *Discourse Concerning the Original and Progress of Satire*, ll. 636–8.

Chapter 5

A good outline of the Exclusion Crisis is provided by Ogg, a longer account by J. R. Jones, *The First Whigs: The Politics of the Exclusion Crisis, 1678–83* (Oxford, 1961). For specific aspects of contemporary politics see J. P. Kenyon, *The Popish Plot* (1972); Tim Harris, *London Crowds in the Reign of Charles II* (Cambridge, 1987), covering much more than its title suggests; J. Miller, *Popery and Politics in England 1660–1688* (Cambridge, 1973); K. H. D. Haley, *The First Earl of Shaftesbury* (Oxford, 1968); Richard Ashcraft, *Revolutionary Politics and Locke's 'Two Treatises of Government'* (Princeton, 1986), which is a detailed account of Whig political thought. For the political verse of the period see *Poems on Affairs of State*, and the discussion by Steven N. Zwicker, 'Lines of Authority: Politics and Literary Culture in the Restoration', in *Politics of Discourse*, edited by Kevin Sharpe and Steven N. Zwicker (Berkeley, 1987) pp. 230–70. On Dryden's politics, besides Zwicker's two books, there is an important article by Phillip Harth on 'Dryden in 1678–1681: The Literary and Historical Perspectives' in *The Golden and the Brazen World: Papers in Literature and History, 1650–1800*, edited by John M. Wallace (Berkeley, 1985) pp. 55–77. W. K. Thomas' *The Crafting of 'Absalom and Achitophel'* (1978) discusses Dryden's poem in the light of contemporary pamphlets.

1. Thomas Shadwell, *The Medal of John Bayes* (1682) A^r.
2. See Harth, 'Dryden in 1678–1681'.
3. See Wilmer G. Mason, 'The Annual Output of Wing-Listed Titles 1649–1684', *The Library* 39 (1974) 219–20.
4. See R. F. Jones, 'The Originality of *Absalom and Achitophel*', *Modern Language Notes* 46 (1931) 211–18; Caroline Edie, 'Right Rejoicing', *Bulletin of the John Rylands University Library of Manchester* 62 (1979–80) 81.
5. For further details see the notes to the poem in my forthcoming edition of Dryden in the Longman Annotated English Poets series.
6. An exception is Monmouth's journey through the West Country (ll. 682–746), which was dangerous both as a political recruiting drive and as an appropriation of the symbolism of the royal progress. Dryden carefully shows that it was masterminded by Shaftesbury with Machiavellian cunning.
7. George Hickes, *A Discourse of the Soveraign Power* (1682) p. 7.
8. John Nalson, *The Common Interest of King and People* (1677) pp. 117–18.
9. These questions are explored further in my essay 'The King's Two Bodies: Representations of Charles II' (see ch. 3 n. 13).
10. See further Anne T. Barbeau, 'The Disembodied Rebels: Psychic Origins of Rebellion in *Absalom and Achitophel*', *Studies in Eighteenth-Century Culture* 9 (1979) 489–501.
11. 'The Cabal', ll. 87–8, 65–6, 72; in *Poems on Affairs of State* ii 331–2.
12. *A Letter from a Person of Quality, to his Friend in the Country* (1675) p. 3.
13. *A Hue and Cry after Dr. T.O.* (1681).
14. The Jesuit John Warner (himself hardly an impartial witness) in *The History of English Persecution of Catholics and the Presbyterian Plot*, edited by T. A. Birrell, translated by J. Bligh, Catholic Record Society vols 47–8 (1953–5) ii 415–16.

15. *A Hue and Cry.*
16. *Poems on Affairs of State* i 189, 251, 281, ii 343.
17. See Paul Hammond, 'Dryden's *Albion and Albanius*: The Apotheosis of Charles II', in *The Court Masque*, edited by David Lindley (Manchester, 1984) pp. 169–83.
18. Edmund Hickeringill, *The Mushroom* (1682) p. 9.
19. Thomas Shadwell, *The Medal of John Bayes* (1682) pp. 2, 3, 23.
20. Macdonald, *Bibliography*, p. 233.

Chapter 6

The best guide to Dryden's religious writing is Phillip Harth's *Contexts of Dryden's Thought* (Chicago, 1968), which corrects Bredvold's book at some crucial points. Subsequent works include Sanford Budick, *Dryden and the Abyss of Light* (New Haven, 1970) and G. Douglas Atkins, *The Faith of John Dryden* (Lexington, 1980). For one aspect of the religious context see John Spurr, '"Rational Religion" in Restoration England', *Journal of the History of Ideas* 49 (1988) 563–85. The church to which Dryden converted is well described by John Bossy in *The English Catholic Community 1570–1850* (1975). For the religious thought of Dryden's plays see the headnote to chapter 3. For *Religio Laici* see Elias J. Chiasson, 'Dryden's Apparent Scepticism in *Religio Laici*', *Harvard Theological Review* 54 (1961) 207–21; Thomas J. Fujimura, 'Dryden's *Religio Laici*: An Anglican Poem', *Publications of the Modern Language Association of America* 76 (1961) 205–17; and K. W. Gransden, 'What Kind of Poem is *Religio Laici*?', *Studies in English Literature* 17 (1977) 397–406.

1. Folger Shakespeare Library, Washington; copy no. D2212.
2. For a definition of 'scepticism' in this sense see Harth, pp. 1–31.
3. Macdonald, *Bibliography*, p. 33.
4. Published in French in 1678; the English translation was by Henry Dickinson, to whom this part of *Religio Laici* is addressed.
5. Harth, p. 203.
6. *The Diary of John Evelyn*, edited by E. S. de Beer (1959) p. 839.
7. For examples see *Poems on Affairs of State* iv 73–90; attacks printed after the Revolution of 1688 include Tom Brown's *The Reasons of Mr. Bays Changing his Religion* (1688) and *The Late Converts Exposed* (1690).
8. See Paul Hammond, 'A Source for *The Hind and the Panther* in a Beast Fable from the Exclusion Crisis', *Notes and Queries* 227 (1982) 55–7.
9. The privileging of speech over writing is part of a long philosophical tradition, for which see Jacques Derrida, *Of Grammatology* (1976).
10. Dryden's translation: 'The First Book of *Ovid*'s Metamorphoses', ll. 308–20.

Chapter 7

There are three books on Dryden's translations: William Frost's early essay *Dryden and the Art of Translation* (New Haven, 1955); Judith Sloman, *Dryden: The Poetics of Translation* (Toronto, 1985), which has some good local observations but is less convincing on the significant arrangement of the translations; and Cedric D. Reverand II, *Dryden's Final Poetic Mode: The 'Fables'* (Philadelphia, 1988), which is alert to the guiding ideas in the *Fables* but neglects the relation of the poems to their originals. David Hopkins' *John Dryden* also emphasises the importance of the translations. A pioneering article on Dryden's methods as a translator was J. McG. Bottkol, 'Dryden's Latin Scholarship', *Modern Philology* 40 (1943) 241–54. Stuart Gillespie discusses 'The Early Years of the Dryden-Tonson Partnership' in *Restoration* 12 (1988) 10–19. There are a number of worthwhile articles on particular translations. H. A. Mason has a series in *The Cambridge Quarterly* on Dryden's translations of Horace; on *Epode* II: 'The Dream of Happiness', 8 (1978) 11–55 and 9 (1980) 218–71; on *Ode* III xxix: 'Living in the Present', 10 (1981) 91–129; and on *Ode* I ix: 'The Hallowed Hearth', 14 (1985) 205–39. The Lucretian translations in *Sylvae* are studied by Paul Hammond in 'The Integrity of Dryden's Lucretius', *Modern Language Review* 78 (1983) 1–23. David Hopkins writes on 'Nature's Laws and Man's: The Story of Cinyras and Myrrha in Ovid and Dryden', *Modern Language Review* 80 (1985) 786–801, and on 'Dryden and Ovid's "Wit out of Season"', in *Ovid Renewed*, edited by Charles Martindale (Cambridge, 1988) pp. 167–90. Emrys Jones discusses 'Dryden's Sigismonda' in *English Renaissance Studies Presented to Dame Helen Gardner* (Oxford, 1980) pp. 279–90. Tom Mason writes on 'Dryden's version of *The Wife of Bath's Tale*' in *The Cambridge Quarterly* 6 (1975) 240–56. See also Paul Hammond's articles cited in ch. 2, headnote and n. 2.

1. See Prologue, n. 1.
2. *Iliad* I 78–83. These are my adaptations of the Loeb translations.
3. *Iliad* I 122.
4. *Iliad* I 158–60.

Epilogue

1. 'W.G.' in *The Gentleman's Magazine* 15 (1745) 99.
2. William Congreve, writing in 1717; quoted from *Dryden: The Critical Heritage*, pp. 264–5.

Index